To: Will Bates
From: First Baptist Church

May God bless you
for teaching His
Word.

"Tim Clayton skillfully weaves together the Christmas story, his personal story, and our own, helping us see it all as God's weaving. A perfect Advent reflection."

Msgr. Charles M. Murphy
Author of *The Spirituality of Fasting*

"It's refreshing to find a deceptively simple book of devotion that gets back to the heart of the Christian pilgrimage as a romance. We are part of a love story, and we learn to love by being willing to live into deep questions.

In the monastic community where I was trained as a priest, we were told constantly that God is madly in love with us and wants us to come home. This is a book about that homecoming—a timely one in an age of estrangement. But how are we to read the drama of Christmas? Primarily, through the door of amazement, reading the stories with the eyes of love. This is a generous book—a true celebration of the Good News."

Alan Jones
Dean Emeritus
Grace Cathedral, San Francisco

Exploring Advent

with Luke

Four Questions for Spiritual Growth

Timothy Clayton

ave maria press AMP notre dame, indiana

Translations of scripture made by the author are noted as AT (author's translation).

Otherwise, scripture quotations are from the *New Revised Standard Version* Bible, copyright © 1993 and 1989 by the Division of Christian Education of the National Council of Churches of Christ in the USA. Used by permission. All rights reserved.

© 2012 by Timothy Clayton

Founded in 1865, Ave Maria Press is a ministry of the United States Province of Holy Cross.

www.avemariapress.com

Paperback: ISBN-10 1-59471-304-9 ISBN-13 978-1-59471-304-0

E-book: ISBN-10 1-59471-356-1 ISBN-13 978-1-59471-356-9

Cover image © Richard Griffin / Alamy.

Cover and text design by Katherine Robinson Coleman.

Printed and bound in the United States of America.

Library of Congress Cataloging-in-Publication Data is available.

Contents

It is a cold December morning and I am sitting in a nineteenth-century stone church surrounded by rattling cornfields. The priest, who ministers to far-flung rural parishes, is delivering a surprisingly fiery Advent homily against the secularization of Christmas. He's worked himself into a fine rant, but I can't really blame him. The blatant commercialization, the unnecessary stress, the unrealistic expectations that lead to holiday depression—he's right, the whole thing's become a sorry mess. Finally he throws up his hands, leaving us with a metaphor I've never been able to forget: "It's a fox farm out there!"

Thank heaven, then, for this book, which is meant to liberate us from fox-farm Advents. This year, instead of reluctantly acquiescing to the norm, we're invited to experience the season in a whole new way. We are shown how to read Luke's age-old nativity story from a more engaged perspective, one that can reinvigorate our preparation for Christmas.

Drawing on a lifetime of pastoral teaching, Timothy Clayton teaches us how to really *hear* the many questions posed by Luke's characters, whether these be elderly Zechariah's doubtful query (Are you talking about *my* wife, God?), a young virgin's astonished cry (But how can this be?), or the diplomatic inquiries of foreigners who've spotted a mysterious new star in the East. Through illustrations rooted in personal experience, he demonstrates how to respond to these questions within the circumstances of our own lives (What am *I* being called to seek? What am *I* being called to relinquish? What am *I* being called to do?). And then he leads us into the heights and depths of Luke's great Christmas canticles, where hope eternally abides.

At least once each Advent season, I think of that anguished priest, so determined to make us see what we've lost. I wish I could find him and give him this book.

Paula Huston
Author of *Simplifying the Soul*

Engaging
the Story
of This
Great Season

Christmas is the season that promises to touch our deepest needs and to meet our deepest longings; it is the story of God remembering us, caring about us, and squeezing himself into time and space, drawing near, even as one of us. If we are remembered, loved, and known by the One who is our ultimate source of life and destination, who exists beyond all time and constraint, then all worries, fears,

1

and anxieties melt away. Or should melt away, it seems. But is there anyone for whom this is actually the case?

Many folks know the Christmas story and what it is meant to say to us, and they believe these things in some abstract sense; and yet the story does not *live* for them anymore. It has worn thin under the tiresome weight of life. The extra stressors of the season do not help: the cards, the family Christmas photo, the decorating, the office party, the neighborhood party, and the extended family in town or in the home. Much of it all is genuine, but much also feels contrived. Some of it is shared with people who also believe the story and long to experience the depths of its meaning, but many of these events simply serve to dilute the very season which gave them their excuse to get scheduled in the first place; they are social and essentially generic. They do not bring the story to life in our hearts; they make it seem surreal and removed. And all the while, the expense of it all in terms of energy as well as money can feel like anything but a reason to rejoice and a source of hope.

Others perhaps long to believe but simply cannot see how the Christmas story could touch them. Life has had too many unhappy surprises or at least unfulfilled hopes and longings. Or they have made too many choices for which they now carry a load of regrets. The heroes and heroines of this story are too pure, too perfect, too pristine; my story could not weave into this story, they feel. Shame scares them off, or unmet yearnings are too painfully sensitive. As this great story is told every year, they retreat into the anonymous background of being an "extra." They are around, but are careful to stay in the background.

Other folks are yet another step removed. They wonder that anyone in the modern world still believes this old story. Isn't it rather implausible? Their cynicism sneers that in reality the story lives only as a way to drive the consumer economy and provide distraction through the turn to bleak winter.

These struggles weary us, perhaps even if they are not ours to bear; perhaps someone we love brings them to us, or by his or her mere presence keeps them before us. Maybe one or more of these struggles sting, and we cower in fear. And yet, something deep within us won't give it up.

Well, what if the one who told this story perhaps most beautifully of all also knew and understood these kinds of struggles? What if he wrote the story in a way that was designed to help his readers wrestle with some of these troubles? Could that be? Can the story as written in Luke's gospel still come alive and pull us—our imaginations and our lives—*into* it, as it were? And is this possible without doing violence to the original story or to Luke's intent as author of it?

What if an effective tool to bring this story to us again as the gift of a living story would not be primarily a how-to book on simplifying the season? Though simplifying would seem an attractive way to go and would no doubt be helpful, still, a how-to book threatens only to add to the stresses it tries to alleviate; there's yet more to sort out. On the other hand, what if weaving our stories into this story is not truly accomplished by an (yet another) attempt to find adjectives grand and piquant enough to match the size of the season's message and worth? If we could find adjectives pithy enough, that would seem a good thing, for this is a story uniquely touching in all of history. But really there simply do not seem to be any adjectives that truly can carry the weight, and the dogged effort at it only tends to lead to the opposite effect, losing any possible deep connection somewhere in the embellishment.

But here is a beautiful and a simple idea: the way to bring this story back to life and to find my story drawn into it as a living story with texture and depth may be simply to read this story again in Luke's gospel, where it is arguably most beautifully and romantically told, and to sit with God in it, asking questions.

The happy joy of all this is that Advent is a season meant to give us just such a space in our lives—a space for self-reflection, for waiting upon and expecting God to show up and perhaps even to speak to us. Advent is a season of remembering, expecting, and listening for God's presence. And Luke has given us questions and canticles (poetic songs) to lead us—if we dare to go on a journey with him—through a spiritual reading that brings the story to life and intertwines our story with it.

It works like this: Luke was a powerful and deeply effective storyteller. He has long been recognized for his telling of the parables of Jesus and for the narrative quality of his gospel. In fact, the Holy Spirit chose him to write more of the New Testament than any other author.[1] What is less well known and therefore of less spiritual benefit to modern Christians is Luke's use of two other powerful literary rhetorical tools: questions and poetry.

Luke uses questions to pull his reader's imagination more deeply into the story. There are places where Luke chooses only to report that a question was asked, but not to show it asked on the lips of "live" narrative time in the action, so to speak. In contrast, in those places where Luke has a figure in the story ask a question in live narrative time, the question reaches out—off the page as it were—and pulls the reader into the context—often powerfully, but effectively even when only implicitly—as through sympathy or disdain. There is something about the open-endedness of a question that demands reciprocity when spoken in the narrative and therefore engages the reader in the narrative moment and transforms it into a now-living moment for him or her.

For instance, we had been nicely reading along, just following a story from a long time ago in another culture and a far-away land, when suddenly we find a new emotional investment has burst open within us. "Oh, Zechariah felt *that* way when the angel Gabriel appeared and spoke to him? How *could* he? How *dare* he say that?" Or maybe we feel the opposite: "He's right to demand assurance! How could anyone believe *that*? He'd risk too much! They've suffered enough already." Either way, now the situation is in our heart and our imagination, and we have to figure out who Zechariah was and why he responded as he did. Then we learn about ourselves as well because we are either sympathetic with his response or we are not. Either way, the truth deep inside us is revealed.

As for poetry, Luke uses poetry for the same reasons all poets use poetry: it speaks more deeply than analysis or even narrative is able. It has been noted that Luke's canticles in the birth narrative function the way songs function in a musical; the action pauses as the song leads the audience into deeper reflection, maybe even transporting us through the beauty of the piece. Might that be the reason that perhaps the "Magnificat" (Mary's song, and the second canticle Luke records in his birth narrative) is the single most set-to-music poem of all of history?

So questions and poetry are two literary rhetorical tools that Luke uses adroitly, as inspired by the Holy Spirit. But "wait a minute!" we may protest; the gospel story happened once only and is utterly unique, in a way beyond even how every story is unique. So does it work to weave our stories into it? Yes, because Luke has done this; he has used two literary tools to invite his readers to join in the story in their imaginations. He invites us to see the characters as real people and see our similarities with or differences from these people. Then, as our sympathetic imagination has been engaged, we begin more deeply to appropriate God's great act of Gospel (of the *good news* of his love) to ourselves.

There are four questions directly posed by characters in Luke's gospel before the birth of Jesus. Luke uses these four questions to walk the reader through a process of spiritual preparation for the great event of the birth, moving the reader from a place of potential cynicism or heart-weariness from the realities of life, to a place of praise and anticipation at the reality of the love and power of God. After the questions have begun their work, Luke introduces poetical reflections (the canticles) that guide the reader's imagination in wrestling with the questions.

This book is a guide along the spiritual pilgrimage laid out in Luke 1—and it is meant to facilitate your encounter with the four questions and poetry of Luke's birth narrative and suggest ways you may interact with them—but ultimately this interaction is for you to do personally with God, of course. The pace of the pilgrimage is designed to be roughly one chapter a week, slow enough to allow for reflection and contemplation. There is one question for each of the four weeks of Advent, then follows one short chapter on Christmas Eve or soon thereafter, and one chapter during the twelve days of Christmas. The journey concludes with space to take up whatever has been revealed or whatever conviction or calling may have come.

Grace and peace to you as you begin your Advent pilgrimage.

Do I Dare to *Open Myself* to God?

There are perhaps few things as difficult for us to handle as disappointment. We fancy ourselves modern people, the products of a wealthy, technologically advanced—and powerful—Western culture. We've invested heavily in the dream of a world in which one shouldn't really have to put up with things not being up to a certain level, and shouldn't have to face an unsatisfying, or painful, or unjust life—truly to find ourselves stuck just having to face disappointment— without having recourse to some alternative.

So when disappointment comes, we protest. We're simply not used to it; we're used to being offered choices. We're used to being able to complain that such and such is "simply not acceptable," it does not meet our expectations of service, comfort, or convenience.

When that doesn't work, there's always denial, or "redefining myself" and "making my world work for me": a retreat into a universe no larger than my own mental and social constructs.

It is natural, of course, that we shouldn't *like* disappointment—it is inherent in the word itself that it is a lacking, an opportunity lost, a sense of life's not being all it was meant to be. The ripple effects of our original parents' fall from perfection and their removal from the Garden are ubiquitous and pervasive, and each of us since has done our own part in keeping those ripples energized and on the move. Their vast wake of consequences seen and unseen carry on, disrupting our lives and beyond.

So disappointments come. In many shapes and sizes, for reasons we can sort out and for seemingly no reason we can discern. For many in our empowered and privileged culture, the disappointments of our lives form the biggest block to a living, vibrant relationship with God. Maybe God is out there somewhere, as the pop song from a few decades back suggests, watching "from a distance"; but we would be slow to believe that God could be intimate, near, dear, *and* powerful, able, active. Or perhaps we would even be angry should we find out God is near and wants to be known intimately. We'd have a few things to clear up with him before we'd let that happen!

Perhaps, were we to be honest with ourselves, we would have to admit that the whole notion scares us deeply. If God's presence became real to us in a deep and true way, we'd have to face the things we've denied or shoved down or learned to keep at arm's length, tangential; and we would have to wrestle with God over how all this fits together, and how we would go on with him coming alongside, present, day after day, week after week, and on and on.

Advent is about God's presence: it is about remembering his past presence in history, looking forward to his presence wonderfully to come in triumph in the future, and also seeking to experience his presence with us now, in our lives in the present moment. Perhaps it is this last one which is the most challenging to believe. Perhaps we may need to clear the ground a little in order to be able to experience God's presence in a way that seems real and personal, and yet is also the way that he would love for us to know him and enjoy his love and intimacy.

During graduate school in theology my dream was to become a professor of American history at a top-notch university or college. I had it all sorted out with a master plan: after a theology degree I would study history, get a doctorate, and then take my theological grounding and historical expertise and be a light for the Gospel on a major campus somewhere.

Everything seemed to be lining up; I was doing well and enjoying my studies. I stumbled upon a wonderful and undiscovered historical gem—a story of Christians in the American South seventy or so years *before* the Civil War who had been led by their faith in Jesus Christ to repent of their participation in slavery. They freed their slaves, faced economic deprivation, and were forced to move to Kentucky and Ohio, the frontier of their day, to make a new start on a smaller scale. This was a powerful, beautiful, and encouraging story of the Holy Spirit leading the people of God to act justly, to love mercy, and to walk humbly with their God. This was a story begging to be told, and of the sort that writes tickets to graduate studies in history.

It was an untold story when I found it; as far as I know, it still is.

I researched doctoral programs. I visited a popular, much-published professor at an august and renowned university in England. I visited a celebrated and decorated professor in the relevant area of history at an American Ivy League school. They were both interested. I sorted out a few fine but slightly lesser schools where I would also apply, and a so-called safety-valve school.

Perhaps you suspect where this is going. My glorious career in American history never got off the ground. I was rejected by all of the programs, from England to Ivy League to safety valve. I was caught shorthanded: a beautiful young wife, two very young little girls, and a flood of terror in my heart. Was I going to fail them already, when I was just barely out of the gate?

Worse, if possible, where was God in the midst of all of this? The sense I had known of things seemingly all leading in this direction, the sense of the happy hand of Providence leading me to discover this hidden gem of a story—a story with a sense of moral imperative that it must be told—was swept away. It all hit me like the proverbial pile of bricks: the hours I had put into research and writing, the money it had cost to go visit the relevant libraries, the exuberance of the conversations with those excellent professors, and the confidence and encouragement my dear family had expressed and given to me.

It came time to move from our housing on campus; I had no answer, so we packed up a truck, and my father came and helped me drive the sixteen hours to my parents' house, back to my childhood home, where my little family spent the next six months.

In my years of pastoral work since then, certainly I have met people whose disappointments in life have cut more deeply and wounded more permanently. But at the time, disappointment joined with shame and regret and a terrifying, disorienting sense that, though I had just finished a degree in theology with high honors at a fine school, I no more could sort out the voice and direction of God—could in no real sense discern the difference his presence made in my life—than I could have tracked and hunted a bear barefoot with a spear, as my long-distant Cherokee forefather perhaps had done.

All that work, all that energy, all that dreaming had come up barren, and all I had to show for it now was a period of desperately passionate prayer.

Zechariah's Question

Luke begins his story of God's presence coming to be among us as a man in the surprising manner of introducing us to a husband who has been crying out in desperate prayer over a disappointment that is wounding his wife and his life. In beginning this way, Luke opens the gate and welcomes all of us, wounded and wondering, to come into the story as a living story still today.

Some of the common translations flatten or dilute aspects of Luke's deft touch as a storyteller. For instance, Luke 1:5 more literally begins something to the effect of "It came about in the days of Herod, King of Judea." Luke loves to use the phrase "it came about," and the phrase wonderfully and subtly leads us to feel something of the ethos Luke is trying to create. Ordinary life is going on for ordinary people whose lives are only remembered or marked, as it were, by reference to the rulers, the powerful, and the famous. These common people pass their days in inconspicuous and seemingly inconsequential lives. The rulers rule and believe that they make and mark the days and the world. But in reality, beyond the veil and in the heavens, something wonderful has been put into motion; and at the right, crucial moments, it breaks through. Things come about via a Weaver few realize is weaving. Even among those who are involved, none see the whole of the divine tapestry. "It came about"—when used this way by Luke, the sentence is sort of like "once upon a time" meets history—it is both fairy tale and actual, historical. It is "once upon a time" woven from heaven into a particular time.

So it is for the couple we meet. Zechariah is a priest, and Elizabeth, his wife, is descended from the order of priests. For them this heritage lives, and they feel it:

> It came about in the days of Herod, King of Judea, that there was a priest named Zechariah, of the priestly division of Abijah. His wife was descended of Aaron, and her name was Elizabeth. Both of them were righteous before God, living blamelessly according to all the commandments and righteousness of the LORD. (Lk 1:5–6, AT)

But in spite of this good heritage, their days are not spent in the joy of a life fulfilled:

> "But they did not have children, because Elizabeth was barren, and both were advanced in the days of their life." (Lk 1:7, AT)

Luke is foreshadowing, sowing a seed of dramatic tension, and he follows it up with his favorite hint that Providence is at work:

> And it came about, while he was serving with his order of priests before God that, according to the custom of the priests, they cast lots and he was chosen to enter into the Temple of the LORD to burn the incense. And all the multitude of the people were outside praying at the hour of incense. (Lk 1:8–10, AT)

A turn to something happy! In the midst of Zechariah's good and upright service comes a day he has long awaited. For what will probably be the only time in his career, the lot falls to him to go into a special, sacred area reserved for the chosen priest to offer the incense for the people around 3 p.m. It will take place in a restricted area—not quite the *most* sacred place in the Temple (the Holy of Holies) but nonetheless a special area, perhaps like a side chapel in a great cathedral, isolated enough to be closed off to the public.[1]

One commentator inserted the phrase "won the privilege" into verse 9: "He won the privilege of entering the sanctuary of the LORD to burn the incense." The phrase is, as the commentator admits, not literal, but it does capture the excitement of the moment. Each of the twenty-four divisions of priests served one week twice a year in the Temple. During their time on duty, lots were used to sort out who took which task. Each morning they would cast four lots, and the winner of the third of those four would have the honor of offering the evening incense. This act was a privileged honor and would typically only come once in a lifetime because once a priest had done it he was ineligible to win that lot again until all the priests of his division had had the opportunity to offer the incense.[2]

It's a big day for Zechariah, and about to get bigger:

> There appeared to him an angel of the LORD,
> standing at the right of the altar of incense.
> Seeing him, Zechariah was troubled and fear
> fell upon him. The angel said to him: "Do not

> be afraid, Zechariah, your prayer has been
> heard." (Lk 1:11–13a, AT)

The angel comes down onto the right side of the altar, a fitting place of honor between the altar itself and the golden candlesticks, and then says what angels pretty much always have to say before they can get on with their business at hand: "Do not fear." Zechariah has been interceding for the people as he offered the incense, and who knows, it may be that God has taken offense at some particularly stubborn aspect of the people's lives, has at last reached the end of his long-suffering patience, and is about to give Zechariah a hard word to deliver to them. Or perhaps Zechariah fears that he has somehow offended God's awesome and complete holiness; it might be called a privilege to enter the particularly holy areas of the Temple, closer to God's unfiltered presence, or it might be called a kind of risk, potentially even perilous.

But it is none of these. It is much happier and much scarier, both at the same time. "Your prayer has been heard," the angel says, and he does not mean Zechariah's official prayers of the incense offering, but rather the cries of his heart. Wonder of wonders, this is a particular and personal visit from the angel; the prayer to which the angel is referring is Zechariah's personal, intimate prayer for his wife and their desires to add to their family.

And so the angel continues, in beautiful speech that some have described as being almost poetic:

> Do not fear, Zechariah, your prayer
> has been heard.

> And your wife, Elizabeth, will bear a son to
> you, and you will name him John.
> He will be joy and gladness to you, and many
> will rejoice at his birth. (Lk 1:13–14, AT)

John means, "God has given grace." This son will be a gift
of grace, leading to joy and gladness for the parents and
indeed for many. Only not right away! The angel goes on,
and the rest of what he says matters, of course:

> For he will be great before the LORD, and
> will not drink wine or strong drink,
> and he will be filled with the Holy Spirit
> even from the womb,
> and many of the sons of Israel will turn to
> the LORD their God.
> He will go before his face, in the spirit and
> power of Elijah,
> to turn the hearts of the fathers to the
> children and the disobedient to the wisdom
> of the righteous,
> to prepare a people ready for the LORD. (Lk
> 1:15–17, AT)

In fact, one might say that the rest of what the angel
said is the better part of the point; certainly in terms of
the overall story it would seem to be. It is all foreshadowing what John the Baptist's life and ministry will be and
accomplish, and it is both crucial and amazing in all that it
means. Much of what the angel says comes from or fulfills
major messianic prophecy in Malachi: "See, I am sending

my messenger to prepare the way before me, and the LORD whom you seek will suddenly come to his temple" (Mal 3:1a). And here is the seminal word at the end of Malachi's prophecy, which caused the people of Israel to be always on the lookout for one like and in the spirit of Elijah:

> Lo, I will send you the prophet Elijah before the great and terrible day of the LORD comes. He will turn the hearts of parents to their children and the hearts of children to their parents, so that I will not come and strike the land with a curse. (Mal 4:5–6)

But for all the meaning and amazement of the second part of Gabriel's message, and for the delightful promises of the joy and gladness the son would bring—this "gift of grace"—I can't help wondering if Zechariah heard anything after that first bit, about his wife Elizabeth bearing him a son. His response would seem to indicate that he did not, and perhaps who would have? Who can blame him? At least, so we say. Surely we can identify with Zechariah.

Who knows, but maybe during the couple of seconds it took the angel to finish his message—after that bit about Elizabeth bearing a son—instead of listening, perhaps Zechariah calculated his response. Whatever the reason— quickly calculating, just plain subconscious, or something else—Zechariah had received the best news he could possibly have hoped for, and it was more than he could handle.

So it is here, at this crucial hinge in the drama Luke has been building as he reports this scene, that the question comes. And Zechariah said to the angel: "How can I know this? I am old, and my wife is advanced in her days" (Lk 1:18, AT).

How can I *know*? Consider: what started out as such a great day, one about which he couldn't wait to tell Elizabeth when he got home, has taken a shocking turn. What to do now? All the nights she'd cried herself to sleep. All the nights she'd chosen not to bring it up again, because she realized how tired he was of hearing it. All the times in the village she'd passed the younger married women who had children, and seen the tender scenes of mother and child . . . and he's going to go home and raise her hopes higher than ever before, at their age?

It just seemed too good to be true. Zechariah just cannot quite get himself beyond his disappointments and into full trust. His question is absurd, given the immediate circumstances. The angel is present and speaking to him, and normally a visitor journeying all the way from heaven should be enough; but when we are disappointed and hurting we are sometimes less than rational. Zechariah's question could more literally be translated, "According to what can I know this?" He's looking for further special assurance, some sign, some confirmation on his terms, rather than what has come out of the blue, as it were, an utter surprise.

Yet for all the sympathy we may feel toward Zechariah, it seems the angel does not agree with us. "And answering, the angel said to him: 'I am Gabriel, I stand in the presence of God and I have been sent to speak to you and to proclaim to you this good news'" (Lk 1:19, AT).

An angel is a messenger of God. The word "angel" is basically the Greek word for messenger. And this angel, Gabriel, gives Zechariah only this satisfaction: he stands before God, or in the presence of God. *Presence* is the only answer Zechariah gets. From Gabriel's perspective this is sufficient; it is not necessary to diminish God's honor in any way by offering more. Full trustworthiness is implicit. It is a moment that calls to mind God's answer to Moses's question at the burning bush: "Who shall I say sent me?" In other words, "On whose authority am I to act?" Answer: "I am." And that is considered enough, without being intended as terse; it simply is sufficient.

So Gabriel continues,

> "I am Gabriel, I stand in the presence of God and I have been sent to speak to you and to proclaim to you this good news. And behold, you will be silent and not able to speak until the day this one is born, for not believing my words, which will be fulfilled in their time."
> (Lk 1:19–20, AT)

The name "Gabriel" means "God has shown himself strong," and apparently God gave Gabriel authority to act out that strength. Rather than showing the impotence Zechariah fears, Gabriel shows God's power immediately, as he takes Zechariah's voice away. Origen, an African Christian theologian in the middle of the third century, had an especially acute eye for catching the symbolic meanings of things. He noticed the poignant irony between the coming son's calling and the current father's chastening: "For his want of faith with regard to the birth of the voice, he is himself deprived of his voice."[3]

It is true enough as well that it would not do to have a spiritual leader out sowing seeds of doubt among the people; as a priest Zechariah has authority in God's name before the people. God is determined that Zechariah will not be able to unravel the weaving begun in the greater story, of which Zechariah's situation is a thread. In the spiritual realm there is a mysterious principle that words have power. There is an amazing dignity given to us such that what we say has power—our *words* actually matter. Hence Jesus in the Sermon on the Mount makes a rather big deal out of what we might simply dismiss as "name calling," and he seems to go a bit over the top about letting "your yes be yes and your no be no" and anything more—*anything more?*—being of the devil, who is a liar by nature and trade. It seems that if we have to stress it, then at some level in it we are not being honest. So Gabriel nips this problem in the bud, as it were.

There is one more angle on the judgment given to Zechariah. About a century before Origen, Clement of Alexandria saw a kind of mystical purpose to Zechariah's silence relative to that greater story:

> John, the herald of the Word, summoned men
> to prepare for the presence of God, that is, of
> the Christ. And this was the hidden meaning
> of the dumbness of Zacharias, which lasted
> until the coming of the fruit which was fore-
> runner of the Christ—that the light of truth,

> the Word, should break the mystic silence
> of the dark prophetic sayings, by becoming
> good tidings.[4]

Zechariah has spoken from his heart, but he has also overreached himself. By God's great mercy, though, Zechariah is merely chastened; he is not abandoned nor truly hurt, and there are reasons and roles that his chastening is to play. Beyond the symbolic, practical, or mystical aspects of the judgment passed upon Zechariah, the judgment itself turns out to be exactly what, in deep reality, he needs: a little forced gestational silence. For a priest, the voice is a crucial asset, an indispensable tool. To lose one's voice is to lose power and the ability to lead. Zechariah would be giving much less counsel to others in the days to come, would be sharing fewer of his opinions while sitting by the city gate, and would have a lot more going on inside than he would be communicating. He was put in a position such that he had the opportunity for reflection, and just possibly, through that, for renewal, that he might come to believe again, and he might be ready for what was to come. We will meet Zechariah again later in our Advent journey and learn something of the fruit of his gestation.

But in the meantime, as Zechariah's drama goes on in the Temple, the people are outside waiting for him to come out and give them the concluding blessing so they will know their prayers have been offered and all is well.

> And the crowd was waiting for Zechariah and
> marveled at how long he was in the Temple.

> When he came out he was not able to speak to
> them, and they recognized that he had seen a
> vision; and he was making signs to them and
> remained unable to speak. (Lk 1:21–22, AT)

By this point Luke has welcomed us into the great story
that is beginning to unfold, and has reached off the page
to draw our hearts into it. That done, now his telling of the
scene becomes efficient and compact. Six of seven scenes
in Luke's telling of the story of the birth of Christ close
with a departure. It is another clue Luke uses to help his
readers begin to sense that Providence is knitting this all
together from beyond what any of the individual characters
can see or realize. Zechariah's time on duty is over; he's off
back home, and this scene is wrapping up. There is just one
miniscene Luke needs us to see before he moves to the next
major scene with its own question. It is a heartwarming
closure that is also a beginning: a miracle pregnancy to old
people—life begins again, one era closes, another arrives,
and against all hope there is a new start of life:

> And when it was that the days of his service
> were fulfilled, he went to his home. After
> those days his wife, Elizabeth, conceived and
> put herself in seclusion for five months, say-
> ing, "Thus the LORD has done to me in these
> days, when he watched over me to take away
> my disgrace among men." (Lk 1:23–25, AT)

This miniscene both wraps up this scene and fore-
shadows what will come a little later. Luke gives us just a

glimpse inside Elizabeth's heart and mind, and the hints are that Elizabeth seems to know better how to handle such a great blessing: she chooses a period of gestational solitude for herself, with deep gratitude and a sense of expectation. We will meet her again as well, when she poses the third question of our Advent journey, but for now Luke is just giving clues, setting that stage.

Our Question

"How will we know this is so?" How does Zechariah's question speak to us today? Is it a question we also would have asked, or do ask in our own circumstances when we sense the movement of God in our lives?

I felt it when I was stuck back at my parents' house with my wife and two young daughters, wondering whether I'd missed God's call for my life. I didn't know it, but what I needed was a kind of gestational solitude and silence if I were to be able once again to trust God's presence and promises to be real.

Alas, like Zechariah and Elizabeth, my wife showed more sense than I did. She insisted I go with a mission team of a major Christian relief organization for a brief visit to Kosovo in the immediate aftermath of the conflict there in the late 1990s. The relief organization was sending in construction teams to reroof burned-out homes and was racing against the arrival of winter and the snows. It seemed crazy to me; surely I should be spending every waking hour doing any- and everything to figure out what I could do, not flying halfway around the world making hardly an ounce of difference in a situation much larger than what I could truly affect. But somehow she knew, so I went off to a season of gestational silence and solitude, and it saved me.

It saved me in part because it restored a sense of perspective, of courage, and of proportion. There was a pastoral job I had dearly wanted before I left, but deep down I knew it really did not suit; once I got back I told them to forget it. But most deeply it saved me because I rediscovered *presence*, God's presence, during those autumn weeks in Kosovo, whether it was in periods of working alone on various jobs during the days, or sitting in silence during the evenings after the work, or in conversations with salt-of-the-earth men on the team—who were just there to put a shoulder to it but were led to ponder what it all might mean—with whom I realized that saying less was saying more.

A few weeks after I returned, I heard from another church, this one in the Washington, DC, area. It was a large parish with many exciting ministries and among its members top-level professionals working in government, non-profits, and legal fields. It was a place with a wide reach of relationships and a depth of resources. It was, and remains, a community of dynamic faith and deep prayer, of the expectation that Jesus's ongoing life matters, not only on the first Easter Sunday of Resurrection and not only in the great Day of Acknowledgement to come, but every day for every person who calls out to Jesus in faith or in desperation. I had discerned four specific areas of ministry in which I felt I would be able to focus should I find what seemed the proverbial perfect situation. I nearly fell out of my chair when I read their job description; it was the four areas, precisely.

Just a few months earlier, it would have seemed too good to be true. Now it was still a stretch to my faith but not an impossible one; the interview felt more like a meeting of old friends than like an inquiry. It was as if we were simply picking up an earlier conversation that had been left unfinished. We laughed and we reflected seriously together, and the outcome seemed obvious, even to me. The five years Cheryl and I spent there were grand, and the Lord even added a son to our family for good measure.

That was a significant crossroad in my life. There are others—some smaller, some also large, and some just different in other ways. All of them tempted me to demand proof of God's love, trustworthiness, faithfulness, and commitment to our relationship—and most of all, to his *presence* in my life.

You will have your own crossroads, as does everyone.

The Challenge of the First Week

There is a temptation to bang our heads against the crossroads, to try to double our efforts to sort things out, to ask why so loudly and with such heartburn that, even should the answer come down, we'd not be able to pick it up. Another approach would be to take a period of gestational solitude to find silence and ask the Lord to speak, and begin to expect him to, again.

Could it be that from the presence of God our disappointments, fears, anxieties, and all their awful cousins look different? How might they? Or, rather, could it be that from the presence of God the story does not, in fact, end with us or with the circumstances we have felt compelled to accept in spite of ourselves, along with the frustration against ourselves or others?

This may be the place where Zechariah's story, which happened so long ago and in a culture very different from our own, also picks up our stories and begins to weave them in, after we sit in silence and solitude and offer our disappointments up to God.

The challenge of this first step in our Advent journey is to make gestational solitude and gestational silence real this week—to fight for some space and time. Strange as silence and solitude are to our culture and as uncomfortable as they may be to us, our challenge for this week is nonetheless to be determined to carve them out and keep them precious this week before we come to Luke's turn to a seemingly similar but actually deeply different question.

Is There
Room in My Life
for God?

Now we enter the second week of Advent. The commercial machine, of course, has gotten off to an early Christmas-season start and will now kick into overdrive. The hubbub and extra social requirements of the season are upon us. Yet the Advent color is not the popular Christmas red and green; it is purple, as is Lent, the painfully penitential season.

Advent is also a penitential season, the reality of which we have perhaps been reminded of by our rather challenging first step of our Advent journey. Luke's second question in his telling of the story of the birth of Jesus gets a happier response from Gabriel than did the first question, and therefore, perhaps, will give us a little more ease as we bring the question into our own lives. Still, our second step may be no less challenging than the first, just in a different way.

So it was for me when God so graciously rescued me from despair and angst by leading me from disillusionment to a great parish in which to work. My wife Cheryl and I had joked that when we left Boston, where I had been in graduate school, surely we would not move to another place with such horrific traffic and such a high cost of living. For all we did not know about what was to come and for all that looked bleak, at least these two things seemed certain.

The old revival preachers used to warn that God had his ways of keeping us from presumption; I always felt maybe they were over the top a bit about that, but when God moved to rescue me he also moved us to northern Virginia, inside the Washington, DC, beltway. So for all the incredible and obvious blessings—and for all my personal elation as the interviews went well and things began to fall into place—there was one big hurdle remaining. It turned out the parish administrator had been on vacation, out of the country and out of the loop during the rounds of interviews. He returned, and a challenging reality set in: it was a new position and the budget for it was slim at best.

It had so clearly seemed God was weaving all this together; but how could it work out? How could the practical realities of life be resolved? How could the cost of living for my young family possibly be sustained in that intense pressure cooker inside the Beltway?

We had only one car; we had no money. Cheryl had been in graduate school when we married, and I had just returned from a year teaching English in Eastern Europe before Eastern European currencies were accepted on the international market. I was happy to see Cheryl finish her program, of course, but practically it meant I had to wait a year to start graduate school while she finished. I ended up working long-term temporary jobs at the university. During that year our first car died, and we had to replace it. There were undergraduate student loans plus the cost of her graduate school and the looming cost of mine on the horizon. But God was creative and faithful. We both worked through graduate school, one of the other of us as a resident director at colleges near to our programs—a job replete with disturbances and an uncertain schedule and a low salary but which also provided rent-free living—and then Cheryl worked in her field as I began my studies. So by the time we both had finished graduate school, we were broke, but amazingly we also were at even. The only thing we had going for us financially was that we had no debt.

Still, I would be working on a pastor's salary, and a low one at that. During graduate school, credit-card applications boasting high credit limits and guaranteed preapproval would often show up in my school mailbox. Usually I chucked them straightaway, but once I decided to follow up the offer, just to test it out. I called, they asked what my future profession would be, and I told them. I'm not sure the woman on the line actually laughed, but she certainly said flatly that I was denied. I reminded her that the application I had received in the mail indicated in large letters across the top that I was preapproved. She told me to read the fine print at the bottom and hung up.

This experience had not inspired confidence that a bank would be eager to help us. I could not foresee a workable solution. The only housing I figured we would be able to find would likely be so far from the church that we would need a second car, which we could not afford and did not want. Another option was a rental somewhere near a bus line or maybe the Metro. But that felt like a financial trap; the rents were too high to be able to save for a down payment toward a home, and this was the time to be laying some sort of groundwork for the future.

The church referred us to a realtor in the parish; I went along with it because it just seemed the polite thing to do, though I could not see the point. The realtor was kind, knowledgeable, and professional. The first time we met he asked Cheryl to describe her perfect house for this situation. She didn't blink but spouted out: a walk-up within walking distance of the church, near enough to the center of the town for her to be able to walk and take the girls in the stroller to the shops and for me to walk to the Metro stop when I needed to go downtown to meet people. I felt I ought to apologize to the realtor for wasting his time, but something held me back. After all, I had known the helpful effect of Cheryl's discernment before, and I had to admit one other thing: when I had come for the interview and walked down the sidewalk from the hotel to the church, I had had a mystical sense like none I had ever known before. I had the sense of God's blessing and that not only was I on my way to meet the people and the work to which he was calling me but also that this would be my commute to work, this very walk.

But how could that work out? In that city of pomp and circumstance, preoccupied with power and politics, how would the needs of my little family, unknown, well below the radar, without power or publicity, possibly be met?

Mary's Question

Luke's next scene of the great story that the great Weaver was weaving features a person whose life was simple and humble, well below the radar. We immediately note a marked difference from the way Luke's first scene had begun. The difference is striking along these lines of power and politics.

When Luke first began, the story was located in time and history by reference to royalty:

> In the days of King Herod of Judea, there was a priest named Zechariah, who belonged to the priestly order of Abijah. His wife was a descendant of Aaron, and her name was Elizabeth. (Lk 1:5)

Zechariah is a priest, a respected leader from an honored line. When his wife is introduced, we learn of her honorable heritage first, and then we are given her name.

But now that God is on the move, weaving his salvation into time and history, things have changed. The lead into this scene has a much humbler tone from the point of view of the powers of this world: "In the sixth month the angel Gabriel was sent by God to a town in Galilee called Nazareth" (Lk 1:26). The referent of reality has shifted: the sixth month is the sixth month of Elizabeth's pregnancy. Elizabeth's gestation has become the clock keeping the time of the story! The story is kept relative to God's acts and his plans and what he is weaving together. No longer does the reign of a Roman-appointed subking determine the era of time. Now the first actors are God and Gabriel: "The angel Gabriel was sent by God." Reality is determined by the weaving directed from heaven, beyond the veil. And Gabriel is sent to a town so unknown, so removed and remote, that its region has to be specified first. The significance of a place is not set by the empire but by God, who knows the hearts of those who love him, wherever they are.

Finally we get a hint of our heroine: "Gabriel was sent . . . to a virgin engaged to a man whose name was Joseph, of the house of David" (Lk 1:26–27a). But still we are not yet told her name. She is described first by her station in life. She is a virgin. Next, Luke introduces her fiancé, who is named and his important heritage noted, even though he will not figure in this part of the story. Then at the last possible moment before the story comes back to Gabriel on his mission, she has a name: "The virgin's name was Mary" (Lk 1:27b).

She is presented in humble, nearly anonymous light, but then things quickly change. Gabriel's approach to her is decidedly different than what it seems to have been with the honored Zechariah. Apparently God does not keep the same score we do: "And he came to her and said, 'Greetings, favored one! The LORD is with you'" (Lk 1:28).

When Gabriel appeared to Zechariah, he did not offer a greeting. Gabriel's first words came after Zechariah had noticed Gabriel and was afraid, in fact after fear had "fallen upon him." Zechariah seems to have been overcome at the first.

Mary, on the other hand, who is not in the Temple, and does not have the great crowd dependent upon and waiting for her, and is not in the center of the capital city but out in a place so remote and unknown it must be identified by both town name *and* region, Mary, this nearly-anonymous one, gets a gentler or perhaps even a more joyful treatment: "And he came to her and said, 'Greetings, favored one'" (Lk 1:28a). The word "greetings" is the Greek verb "to rejoice." We should not make too much of this word in and of itself for it was simply a standard greeting of the time. However, the word that follows, "favored," contains the same root and is much less common. It appears only two times in the New Testament and only here, in this moment, coupled with the more common "rejoice." Gabriel's message may be shocking, and it will turn Mary's life upside down; but there is no doubt that from the perspective of heaven it is an occasion for joy. His greeting to Mary is warm and evocative and is followed with the greatest assurance any person could receive—the assurance of *presence*: "The LORD is with you" (Lk 1:28b).

Mary, to be fair to Zechariah, does share in a part of his response: "She was much perplexed" (Lk 1:29a). The verb has the same root as the one used first to describe Zechariah's reaction, but the second bit is missing, that part about fear falling upon him. "Zechariah was troubled and fear fell upon him" (Lk 1:12, AT). Unlike what we read about Zechariah, we are not told that she was afraid. Mary, instead, begins to think: "But she . . . pondered what sort of greeting this might be" (Lk 1:29b). Even before they speak there is a noteworthy difference between Mary and Zechariah, a difference emerging from their depths, in their immediate, visceral responses.

But yes, Mary is startled, as anyone would be, and so Gabriel carries on in the manner in which angels are accustomed when they are sent to address mortals: "Do not be afraid."

> The angel said to her, "Do not be afraid, Mary, for you have found favor with God. And now, you will conceive in your womb and bear a son, and you will name him Jesus. He will be great, and will be called the Son of the Most High, and the LORD God will give to him the throne of his ancestor David. He will reign over the house of Jacob forever, and of his kingdom there will be no end." (Lk 1:30–33)

There is wonderful paradox in the message. God knows Mary's heart and has found it to be delightful and open to him, and it is she who will conceive and bear a son whom she is to name nothing less than "God saves." This is no ordinary boy! "He will be great and will be called the Son of the Most High, and the LORD God will give to him the throne of his ancestor David. He will reign over the house of Jacob forever, and of his kingdom there will be no end." And so we arrive back to royalty after all but of a very different sort, even overlooking the miracle for the moment. How would a child of this unknown and unprivileged woman from this remote and nonprestigious village ever possibly live up to all of that?

As with Gabriel's message to Zechariah, his message to Mary is also based in the promises God made to his people from of old. Gabriel's message to Zechariah was based in the messianic prophecy of Micah; his message to Mary seems to be based in God's promises that Samuel was told to tell to David, the one who as king was a kind of foreshadowing of Jesus:

> Now therefore thus you shall say to my servant David: Thus says the LORD of hosts: I took you from the pasture, from following the sheep to be prince over my people Israel; and I have been with you wherever you went, and have cut off all your enemies from before you; and I will make for you a great name, like the name of the great ones of the earth. . . . Your house and your kingdom shall be made

> sure forever before me; your throne shall be
> established forever. (2 Sm 7:8–9, 16)

How did David, the lowly shepherd boy, ever manage to become king and reign with mighty power, except by God working through one who was "a man after my own [God's] heart" (Acts 13:22)?

Yet in spite of this incredible prophecy concerning the son she is to have, it seems Mary shares this with Zechariah as well: for all the beautiful and powerful things that Gabriel says about the coming realization of God's great plan and for all that has been put in motion in the heavens, one wonders if Mary heard much of that part. Like Zechariah, Mary seems perhaps to have gotten stuck on that bit about unexpected conception and birth. But for whatever aspects may be similar between Mary and Zechariah, there is a seemingly subtle nuance that is actually a deep difference of posture or stance.

Zechariah's question was a question of trust and a question of power, in the sense of who held the power in the relationship: "How can I *know*?" Mary's is more innocent, much less self-protecting. It is as if it simply slipped out, simple honest wondering: "How will this be, since I have not known a man?" (Lk 1:34, AT).

So here Luke's second question reaches out into our hearts to work on us in our own lives, to prepare us for the birth. If God wants to move anew in my life and in your life, to draw near and to be more deeply present, to deal with pain and bring salvation—and if, following on last week's spiritual work, I am now willing to risk it—how will this be? After all, some of my troubles have been years in the making and perhaps in the festering. Some of them I have perhaps come in a twisted way to cling to, to see as an integral part of my identity, and to even nurture. It can be useful to carry along a case of hurt. When life gets too challenging, or I meet my own fallibility and I'd rather not admit it, well, I can drag out this or that and display it as an excuse.

All of which is not to deny that some of my troubles and hurts may perhaps have roots that precede my conscious memory or the age of responsibility, when I began to make my own choices. They were done unto me, without my conscious or culpable participation. Or some troubles come from things that do not really have anything to do with me at all, except as a part of the burden of love is inextricably linked to family or old friends, for example. Some it would seem are circumstantially impossible to solve or would need some creative mathematics indeed. Over others I feel I have no control: the other person or people involved are beyond my sphere of influence or no longer invite my input. And so on, and so on. So we join the second question and ask it in our own lives: "God, we would delight in and welcome your salvation for us, but how can it be?"

It is telling and encouraging that Mary's question gets a quite different response from Gabriel than did Zechariah's. God is not put off by questions, as long as they do not call his character into question, or so it seems. Mary gets an answer, and our help as well perhaps comes in Gabriel's response. Notice the themes in the language as Gabriel addresses Mary again: "The angel said to her, 'The Holy Spirit will come upon you, and the power of the Most High will overshadow you; therefore the child to be born will be holy; he will be called Son of God'" (Lk 1:35). It is the language of deeply intense *presence*, when the veil between earth and heaven seems pulled back, and the life of God is especially and particularly manifest.

One of Luke's favorite themes in his two books of the New Testament (Luke and Acts) is God's presence (by his Spirit) among his people, especially the humble, poor, and lowly. One of the common ways Luke expresses this theme is by saying a person was "full of" or "filled with" the Holy Spirit. But this situation is a little different.

The verb here is a strong one—normally in the New Testament when "come upon" is said, the situation is challenging or even ominous; someone is in danger of being "overcome" by adversity or an adversary. But there is another moment in the New Testament when it is the Spirit of God that is described as "coming upon," and that too is another instance in which the promise of this presence is given from heaven's representative, as it were. In Acts 1:8, Jesus promises his disciples that after he ascends into heaven he will send his Spirit to be with them and they will "receive power when the Holy Spirit [had] come upon [them]." It is a poignant moment of the promise of continuing presence in spite of Jesus' physical departure. This moment is like that one, and though it may be overwhelming it is for good by the One who wills good and is good.

But in this situation, as when Jesus promised his Spirit to his disciples in Acts 1:8, God's life-forming, life-creating, life-giving *power* will be the result. Gabriel answered Mary that the Spirit would overcome her, and "the power of the Most High will overshadow you." Describing God's power in Jesus Christ and in those to whom he gave power is another of Luke's favorite aspects of Jesus' life and work. Luke understood God's power to be acting to establish God's kingdom in the midst of time and history, insistently asserting itself against other powers who were comfortable with the way life had been and found Jesus to be an aggravation and a disturbance. Luke loves to draw attention to this power being manifest by God's presence through his Holy Spirit. Gabriel's message shows that this was a part of God's plan from the beginning, as God wove himself into his own creation story, in order to reclaim his creation as his rightful realm in which to reign.

But of course Mary could not have known all of that; it had not yet come about. What she hears is that the power of the Most High would "overshadow" her—another rather intimidating and strong word. The only other time this word is used in the gospels is in each of the synoptic gospels (Matthew, Mark, and Luke) and in the same story in each: the Transfiguration. Jesus had taken Peter, James, and John up to a mountain to pray, and while they were there, Moses and Elijah appeared in a glorious form and began to speak to Jesus to strengthen him for the suffering that he would have to face. As the two ancient men of God were leaving—as the veil between earth and heaven was opened—a cloud came and "overshadowed" the area. The cloud was not merely a distraction, a smoke screen, but was in some manner God's presence come down. Luke writes that "from the cloud came a voice that said, 'This is my Son, my Chosen; listen to him!'" (Lk 9:35).

Peter, James, and John were terrified as they entered the cloud. Would they survive this opening to heaven and the presence of the great and mighty God? But again, of course, Mary could not have known all of this yet either; the point is the intimidating nature of such an encounter with a holy and perfect God.

There is, however, another story in the Bible when the same strong word is used and that is telling for our purposes here. It is in the ancient Greek version of the Old Testament (which would have been the everyday version for Luke and his contemporaries). Only this one time in all the vast pages of the Old Testament is it used in a story as descriptive of direct experience. (There are three other times it occurs in the Old Testament, each of them in poetry and functioning as an image of something else.) And befitting the poignancy of the word, it comes at a dramatic moment in the Book of Exodus, at the climax of the building and setting up of the tabernacle, and as the closing moment of the book.

The people have been rescued from Egypt by God's mighty right hand and outstretched arm, and now God has given them instructions on how to build a travelling home for his presence. He has promised that he will lead them as one leads or carries a child on such a long and hazardous journey. And so they build it, and then, incredibly, the cloud overshadows it *because* the *presence* of God was there in a particularly intense manner, for the salvation and deliverance of his people:

> Then the cloud covered the tent of meeting, and the glory of the Lord filled the tabernacle. Moses was not able to enter the tent of meeting because the cloud *overshadowed* it, and the glory of the Lord filled the tabernacle. Whenever the cloud was taken up from the tabernacle, the Israelites would set out on each stage of their journey; but if the cloud was not taken up, then they did not set out until the day that it was taken up. For the cloud of the Lord was on the tabernacle by day, and fire was in the cloud by night, before the eyes of all the house of Israel at each stage of their journey.[1] (Ex 40:34–38)

Now Mary is to be overshadowed and by that means is to carry the very presence and unique incarnation of God in her womb, in her own person, her own body. Thereby at least in some sense she is to function as a tabernacle, for God will be cloistered there—a paradox that the metaphysical poet John Donne delighted to use for a wit-filled ironic rhyme:

> *Annunciation*
>
> Salvation to all that will is nigh,
> That All, which always is All everywhere. . . .
> Loe, faithfull Virgin, yeelds himselfe to lye

in prison, in thy wombe. . . .
yea, thou art now
Thy Makers maker, and thy Fathers mother,
Thou' hast light in darke; and shutst in little
roome,
Immensity cloysterd in thy deare wombe.[2]

But we are getting a touch ahead of the story. Mary
was dialoguing with an angel—an angel! And the angel
was giving her an answer to her wondering. There is actually quite a lot going on in the few words Gabriel speaks
to Mary; there seems to be an economy to the language of
heaven. Gabriel's response is dense with wonder and amazing allusions to the larger story God was weaving. And we
know the end of the story—at least in terms of Jesus' birth,
life, resurrection, and expected return in glory—and we can
read all of this from armchair-quarterbacking comfort. But
for Mary the whole business was for her rather personal. It
was what we would medically call "invasive." And most
of us are deeply uncomfortable being overwhelmed by
another; we are an independent lot as a culture, and we are
(perhaps appropriately) suspicious of anyone who wants
to get too close, too quickly. If Zechariah's situation was a
trust challenge, surely this is even more so. Yes, certainly,
there is so much that Gabriel has said that is remarkably
assuring and promises incredible blessings: Mary has been
told to rejoice, that she has been favored by God, and that
she has the awesome affirmation that the Lord is with her!
But still, as a faithful Jew, Mary would have known the stories of her people and that the presence of God was nothing

with which to trifle. They understood much better than we
tend to that God's infinite being and his perfect, glory-filled
holiness are different from what we are, and in a way that
matters. If God were to reveal himself completely to any
one of us, we would die instantly, our imperfect selves
obliterated by the fire of utterly pure holiness. The stories
in which the presence of God "overshadowed" were overwhelming for those involved.

So it is a supremely demanding trust move that is asked
of her: to give herself—her body and her future—so completely and fully to God, and to trust that his power would
work and work for good in a way that would not harm her.
All that is necessary is the huge vulnerability that she trust
and make herself open to deep and transforming *presence.*
But before she can respond again to Gabriel, he continues
and gives her encouraging news, which functions as a sign:

> And now, your relative Elizabeth in her old
> age has also conceived a son; and this is
> the sixth month for her who was said to be
> barren. For nothing will be impossible with
> God." Then Mary said, "Here am I, the ser-
> vant of the LORD; let it be with me according
> to your word." Then the angel departed from
> her. (Lk 1:36–38)

Elizabeth is Mary's cousin, and so Mary would have
known Elizabeth's circumstances and struggles over the
years. The personal connection, of course, would have
made Gabriel's words deeply surprising and encouraging to

Mary; God has been weaving the strands of life toward this point for several generations, it seems, which is, of course, not difficult for him. And Elizabeth, we are reminded, is now in her sixth month. Luke directs us in a quick glance toward her "gestational clock," which marked time to open this scene, now also as it draws near its close.

But Gabriel's message has one last word for Mary to ponder. He reminds her that God has done this before: "For nothing is impossible with God" echoes what the LORD said to Abraham after Sarah laughed in derision at the notion that she would, like Elizabeth, bear a son in her old age, way back in Genesis 18:14. That Gabriel would expect Mary to catch the allusion is not a stretch; again, faithful Jews would have been steeped in the old stories of their people, and one may expect young women in particular to have known the stories of the heroines of their past.

So what is needed is that Mary trust and make herself open to deep and transforming *presence*, and thank heaven, she does! She utters what was quickly seen by early Christians to be the ultimate response of the follower of Jesus to God's acting in his or her life: "Let it be done unto me according to your word" (AT). Mary's confession is powerful, and it opened the way in some mysterious manner for the Spirit to bring into being a whole new reality—God incarnate.

We noted in chapter 1 that Luke lets the departures of characters mark the end of scenes in the larger story he is telling. Mary has answered well, and there is nothing left to say. "The angel departed from her."

Our Question

It is quite a story, of course, to say the least. And obviously it is utterly unique in all of history as a supreme moment of God's acting to save. But does that mean that nothing in the story is transferable to us? Is it possible we can learn from Mary's response? Her circumstances were naturally impossible; only a miracle could bring about what Gabriel promised. And yet the Spirit of God had hovered over the chaos in the beginning, and out of that chaos came order, life, and creation; and now the Spirit would come upon her precisely in order that God might gather for himself a new family of people with whom he promises to be forever, and who would forever be with him.

Can the Spirit of God hover over us and do the same, this time for a new—renewed—creation in and of our lives? Where are the places you sense God may be stirring as we have looked at Mary's question and her submission?

I've come to believe that when it happens in my life it is best if I mark the story down and hold on to it. Because it *does* happen; it happens in ways small and sometimes large, and yet later I am prone to doubt it when life turns hard again. But if I've noted it, I can go back and remember. Or at least I can let the evidence in my own handwriting stare me in the face and call my cynicism and hard-heartedness into question.

So there we were—my little family, unknown, not a media feature in Washington, DC, and coming to the big city from having been a few months back in my hometown in North Carolina, a fine place but unknown. It seemed God was on the move, and I had become willing again to risk it, to trust that God may just be present, be with us, and have something worthwhile for me to do in life. Yet now we had hit very real practical challenges, and it did not seem that the math could possibly work.

But we felt God was calling us, and the parish put out the call to ask if anyone could help us. A man in the church offered to live in the basement level of his townhouse and let us occupy the first and second floors as we looked for more permanent housing. A couple in the church heard about us and remembered a low-income townhouse in their neighborhood. It had been a bargain the town council had made with the developer when he went to gain permission to develop the last remaining large open space in the town. This space had been home to an old and beloved elementary school. If he would intersperse four low-income, smaller townhomes into the midst of his upscale townhome development, he could close the deal with them. The terms were that those who bought those four homes had either to be currently living in the town or working for a firm or organization in the town.

Low-income pricing in that area was still high enough to scare; it was basically the same as regular pricing for a fairly large, suburban, single-family house down in my hometown in North Carolina. But these were great little houses! A Kenyan friend who came to visit later remarked that they reminded him of row houses he had seen in London—tall, slender, and stately (well, almost). They were brand new and in the midst of very fine houses. In fact, the developer had felt it was cheaper to use the same fixtures and features in the four low-income homes that he used in the bigger ones. All that stuff was being bought in bulk and shipped to the site anyway; it was easier not to make exceptions. Not surprisingly, three of the four houses were snatched up before they were finished.

But one sat strangely empty well into the first year after the development had opened. The town had not been able to find anyone in the right income bracket that also met the residency or work requirements. But I did work for an institution in the town—in fact, the parish was the oldest institution in the town and had been giving back to the life of the town from the town's very beginning.

Why not at least go see it, we thought. So we did. Our girls were delighted with the springy doorstops and spent the visit flopping them back and forth and giggling. My wife had grown up near one of the great cities of the northeast of our nation and felt that living in a three-story row house would be fun. By the time the visit was over all I knew was that the pressure was on. Would they take a risk on us? The house was listed as "low-income" and even still we were on the low side of their income range. But they were willing to take a look and start the process. Would we ever get through all the red tape?

And so it began. What a long period of waiting and praying—roughly six months. During this time I tried to learn to pray along with Mary: "Let it be unto me according to your word." But it was hard not to grasp at it when I looked at my darling daughters, not that there was anything more I could do.

As God would have it, he was just waiting, it seems, for a significant moment that would help to mark the occasion. God really does have such a tender heart—maybe even somewhat sentimental? We moved in on the weekend of our seventh wedding anniversary—what an amazing gift! I've often figured the house was some kind of compensation God gave my wife for assigning her such an arduous task as being covenant bound to me! I have the suspicion that when we get to heaven Cheryl and Jesus will exchange a knowing wink and then burst out laughing. I'll be the one standing there asking what's so funny.

On the one hand it was just a house, and people buy and sell houses all the time, every day, I know. But not in that town, in that very comfortable, old, quaint, colonial Virginia town inside the Beltway. Not in that town for that price and under such strict constraints of circumstance. We were floored, humbled, and overcome by God's graciousness because we did not and do not believe that the purpose of God's miracles is to give us just what we want. Further, a part of my work in that parish was to take our parishioners—some of them wealthy, some of them powerful, some of them Washington players, so to speak—to visit with our brothers and sisters in Christ in some of the world's toughest places, those living in extreme poverty, or in an HIV+ hot zone, or in circumstances where persecution may and did come. The paradox was not lost on me and provided plenty of fodder for my own pondering in prayer, but at least at that time in our lives God wanted to prove us wrong and defend his freedom to be as generous as he wanted to be, indeed to be unpredictably generous and powerful beyond our wildest dreams—or beyond *my* wildest dreams.

The house was exactly what my wonderful wife had said would best serve our young family's needs: a walk-up within walking distance of the church, close enough for me to walk to the Metro stop when I headed downtown to meet someone for lunch or coffee, and near enough to downtown for Cheryl to walk to the post office or wherever and take the girls in the stroller. And so I still remember the pleasant spring day several months later when I was having a lunch meeting in the trendy outdoors seating of the local upscale Irish pub, and my little daughters happened by. They were trotting in front of the stroller, saw me, and ran over to hug me in joy. Hard to stay focused on business when that happens!

The Challenge of the Second Week

Mary accepted God's favor and presence as the gift that it is. She was available and open to how he wanted to bless and use her. Her question was taken seriously, and the Spirit of the Lord hovered over to form an answer and to give his *presence* to his world in a way that had never been experienced before and would make all the difference for all of us. Does God still work out the seemingly impossible? Can we bring our impossible situations to him for salvation and ask with Mary, "How can this be?" that there could be change for good, beyond our ability to work out? The challenge this second week of Advent is to go into these places in prayer, maybe to journal and record what the Lord shows and says to us, and to hold it in hope, even as we pray with Mary, "Let it be done unto me according to your word."

Luke has now told us about two women who have unexpectedly come to be expecting; in the next scene we see them together.

Does God
Really Want Me?

It has been argued that what makes great leaders and great heroes is perhaps an ability to "keep the plot" in spite of the changes and shifts and surprises of life. To see one's own life and identity as being a part of a larger story lends a sense of purpose and broadens out the base of one's life and work. We are a strand in a great story that began before, lasts beyond, and reaches much wider than the span of any one person, even while each person in the story is dignified because each one's role is crucial to the whole story coming off right. It can be deeply healing to come to see one's self in this way, instead of reduced to being simply the product of our genetics, or perhaps forever hobbled by our mistakes and weighted down under past regrets, or even to see ourselves in sanguine ways that nonetheless are still no larger than we are.

Those who understand their own identity as a part of some larger story paradoxically are freed up to lose themselves fully in the larger story courageously, maybe even recklessly, without holding back. It is even beautiful to them and a great joy; few things in life are as energizing. This is what we begin to see now, in the third scene Luke brings to us, his readers: "In those days Mary set out and went with haste to a Judean town in the hill country, where she entered the house of Zechariah and greeted Elizabeth. When Elizabeth heard Mary's greeting, the child leaped in her womb" (Lk 1:39–41a).

There has been a shift. Instead of seeing beyond the veil to the plans and operations of heaven, we see the two characters who we have so far seen to be faithful and open to God's work. They are caught up in the great story of which their lives have become a part with passion, energy, and the depths of their being. Suddenly a clear, specific, and deeply purposeful calling has come to them, and in the midst of that they are given strength to keep the plot and carry on.

So Mary goes with haste and with purpose to visit Elizabeth in a village somewhere up in the hill country. It is a quiet way of saying that the journey took a bit of work and maybe some courage as well. Then we come again to one of Luke's favorite "signal" phrases: "it came about." Gabriel had told Zechariah that their baby would be filled with the Holy Spirit even from Elizabeth's womb, and the telling moment of that comes with this great energy and great joy that John expresses even prenatally as he leaps. It is a powerful and a delightful image; in the Old Testament the word is associated with the raw and unrestrained joy sometimes expressed by robust, virulent young animal life. Psalm 114 reads, "The mountains skipped like rams, the hills like lambs" (Ps 114:4). In Jeremiah it is written, "Though you rejoice, though you exult . . . though you frisk about like a heifer on the grass" (Jer 50:11). In the book of the prophet Malachi especially, such unbridled joy follows what came to be understood as a prediction of the Messiah: "But for you who revere my name the sun of righteousness shall rise, with healing in its wings. You shall go out leaping like calves from the stall" (Mal 4:2).

The weaving from beyond the veil shows through, even if heaven's messenger is not currently on the stage. John's movement is the only place in the New Testament where this particular word "leaped" appears. The moment when it happened was not lost on these two faithful women, and Luke's care to include this sort of detail brings to life the beauty, the depth of emotion, and the human tenderness in this scene. It is a part of the way he expresses the depth of expectation, not only of babies to come, but even more of God's great story, which has been awoken in these two faithful women. There is a meaningful, intensely purposeful confidence in God's acting among and through them that permeates the atmosphere of this scene, and soft hearts will find it beautiful to behold. So then also "Elizabeth was filled with the Holy Spirit and exclaimed with a loud cry, 'Blessed are you among women, and blessed is the fruit of your womb'" (Lk 1:41b–42). This is shameless joy and unrestrained emotion—the word for "loud cry" usually shows up in the scriptures in unhappy settings, in moments of intense distress, and in visceral responses. The visceral element remains, but here in a terribly happy setting, and Elizabeth just cannot hold it in, so she gives a blessing to Mary.

We met Elizabeth before, at the end of the first scene, but briefly—just enough to give closure to that moment so that the overall story could move forward. Again now, as was hinted that first time we met her, she is deeply sensitive to and in tune with the Holy Spirit and is a strong strand in the overall story coming together. From this wise and spiritually attuned woman comes our third question. We sense right away that as different as the second question (Mary's) proved to be from the first (Zechariah's) so also is this a question of a different sort, and it will take us another step deeper into our spiritual pilgrimage through Advent and toward Christmas, as we seek to open ourselves ever more fully to God's presence with us, in our own lives, even today.

Zechariah's question was skeptical; essentially it was a "prove-it-to-me" challenge. And so, as that question reached off the page and came into us, we too sat in a kind of gestational silence and solitude, waiting upon God to make us able to heal and risk his presence with us again or maybe anew.

Mary's question seemed similar on the surface but was in fact quite different precisely for lacking the skepticism; and Gabriel's response to her showed no judgment whatsoever. But still Mary's question too, like Zechariah's, began with the word "how." Her question was a kind of wondering about how God's power would weave into this life. She was not asking an abstractly intellectual question, of course, because the whole situation was quite personal for Mary and changed her everyday life, but still she too asked a "how?" question. And so, as that question came and pulled our own situation and circumstances into the story, we tried to join her in opening up to the life-giving and restoring work of God's Spirit, trying to learn to pray with her, saying, "Let it be done unto me according to your will, O LORD."

Elizabeth's Question

Elizabeth's question moves us now another step deeper and into a different sort of place. The previous two scenes were similar in that each featured an annunciation; each was a moment of miraculous expectation, and the messenger from heaven gave notice to the people who were most affected as God began to intervene in their lives in particular ways. Now those things are in motion, and the locus of the scene shifts somewhat to the story that is beginning to get momentum here on earth. There is no heavenly messenger but simple people going forward in the joy of finding themselves woven into a larger story. As we have noted, it is powerful to find one's self in that weaving; it is, in fact, a gift, but at the same time it can be overwhelming. And so Elizabeth follows her cry of joy with a pause and a question of self-reflection: "And why has this happened to me, that the mother of my LORD comes to me?" (Lk 1:43).

It is not the easiest question to translate; more literally it would read something like: "And from whence is this, in order that the mother of my LORD might come to even me?" The less literal translation is fine, of course, except that it drops one little bit at the end of the question that is telling and important—"*even* me." Greek personal pronouns have a neat trick about them: they can simply be themselves or they can show emphasis, appear in italics, as it were, simply by adding an epsilon, the Greek letter that became our letter *e*, at the front of the little word.[1] And that is what we have here. The point for us is not to sneak an ancient grammar lesson into a modern moment; the point is that that single little letter gives us a meaningful clue to something beautiful in Elizabeth's heart.

Elizabeth, of course, was not the one whom everyone looked to and waited upon to go into the holy place of the Temple; that was her husband, Zechariah. She was not a public figure or considered important in that sense. She was back in the hill country, keeping house. And yet, even to her, a crucial role in such a great story had come home, literally deep inside her, and with remarkable power and energy. "For as soon as I heard the sound of your greeting, the child in my womb leaped for joy" (Lk 1:44). Or, taking this sentence more literally as well, we would get something like, "Behold, for as the sound of your greeting came about to my ear, the child in my womb leaped for joy." This more literal rendering does not read as easily, but the point is that this sentence also includes the little phrase "came about" that is a kind of a hint of the great divine plan being woven into life; Elizabeth is amazed—humbly, wonderfully astounded to find herself as a strand in the great story whose Weaver is in the heavens. She had perhaps grown accustomed to seeing herself as the one who was barren and therefore was shamed; she carried a burden forever in her mind and baggage in her identity that she could never forget. For her this is a proverbial pinch-me moment—all of that gone and forever done? No wonder she expresses such joy! Her life has had a completely unexpected and astounding reversal, and she is free from the burden of shame she had borne so long, free to live into a story of deepest meaning and consequence.

She recognizes the honor and privilege given to her to be in this story and especially to have her own body hold and nurture one especially designated and chosen by God for reawakening a long-dormant hope. John will be the renewal of the prophetic voice, which had gone silent for some four hundred or so years; and because the One to follow John would be the point of so much of the prophecies—the Messiah—John would also come to be seen as the last of the prophets. Jesus himself would say later in Luke's gospel that "among those born of women no one is greater than John" (Lk 7:28).

Elizabeth had no idea her life could mean so much, and so she asks, "Who am I?" that all this goodness and these great things should happen in and through her. Whether we are constantly weighted down by it or only think about it in moments of deep personal honesty, we each know the reasons why it seems that it should not be *us* that God would choose: someone else is smarter, someone else has made fewer poor choices in life, someone else is more charismatic, someone else has more patience, and so on and so on. And yet God chose Elizabeth, and for various other purposes he chooses us. Even us!

Our Question

"Why has such goodness happened to me?" Granted, our lives will never be such a major part of the drama of salvation as Elizabeth's was. Those events are, as we have noted, unique and grand on a scale never to be repeated. Yet again, as with Zechariah and with Mary, the question still comes off the page and engages us deeply; it is still transferable to us and our situation, whatever our situation is and however slight or mundane it may seem. Maybe our contribution will never be recorded for the generations to come to read and remember; maybe it will only involve "small" miracles or the more "natural" miracles that seem to come about as a kind of synergistic effect of God's presence with us. Maybe it will involve "only" loving people who are themselves not known or maybe not even particularly appreciative. Really, it is no matter. Are

we still able to see a plot and to grasp our role as a part of
the heavenly weaving? And if we are, is it not an amazing
privilege? And does the fact of the privilege of God calling us to worthwhile service not in and of itself work to
begin to dissolve our nagging or dominating self-doubts
and regrets? God made us and gifted us to serve in ways
that are real and that matter.

There is a way to ask Elizabeth's question with the
joy and laughter that one can so easily imagine on her
countenance as she greeted Mary. Yes, we are honest with
ourselves about our failings and regrets, but they do not
dominate us; and in the midst of it all, God's love brings
a delight into the present moment. We have a role to play
as God's beloved (*even* us!), and this begins to become
our identity. We too may find that we are more able to
"keep the plot," to have an energy and a joy that transcend
the everyday challenges, and to see our lives caught up in
God's great acts and story. Eventually we find ourselves
so aware of God's presence that we forget to worry or to
doubt ourselves or to expend energy pondering ourselves
overmuch at all—a happy freedom!

That is the place where Mary and Elizabeth were, and
it is a good place to be, as Elizabeth confirmed to Mary:
"And blessed is she who believed that there would be a
fulfilment of what was spoken to her by the LORD" (Lk
1:45). This line reads like a summary, as if Luke is starting
to wrap up this scene; and in terms of the action he is. But
not so fast! Now that the first two scenes are past—the
scenes of the messenger from beyond the veil, bringing

annunciations—and the human characters are playing their roles, as it were, and things are picking up momentum and moving forward, the narrative gives pause for a new literary method of reflection. Amid all the (faithful) activity and (wonderfully) unrestrained emotion, we must not miss the import of what is happening. Luke's gospel here and in the next three scenes is somewhat like a musical—as the plot thickens and the audience comes to the edge of their seats, the conductor cues the orchestra and the audience is asked to hold their curiosity in order to reflect on the larger meaning of the plan that is unfolding. In each of these scenes someone speaks an inspired poem that may also become a song—a canticle.

The Canticle of Mary

This first canticle is Mary's song, the "Magnificat." This poem perhaps has been set to music more than any other. *The Catholic Encyclopedia* holds that "almost every great church composer has worked often and zealously on this theme."[2] Johann Sebastian Bach's "Magnificat" in D major, BWV 243, is considered one of his major works; Mozart, Vivaldi, and Rachmaninoff are among those who composed settings. Going back at least as far as St. Benedict in the sixth century, the "Magnificat" has been sung or spoken each evening by monks and nuns and lay people in far reaches of the globe, as they have gathered for Vespers or Evening Prayer. From the greatest composers and voices in the world's most august and renowned music halls and cathedrals, to the smallest gatherings, anonymous to history and simply marking the end of yet another mundane day, and even to individuals at prayer, communing with God alone, this poem has been sung or spoken as a record of God's great act as these two humble women shared an intimate bond of joy in a remote home in the Judean hills. Who could have known?

It is not the easiest poem to sort out; scholars debate whether it is made up of an introduction, two major stanzas, and a conclusion or composed of three stanzas; and there is no agreement either on precisely how to understand the complex play of words and concepts. The "Magnificat" is fascinating and quite a puzzle in that sense, but through it all the core message remains. A simple way to appreciate the core message without trying to sort out the complexities is to take it as beginning with Mary's personal reflections and reasons to praise God, and then widening the lens to take in the bigger picture of God's faithfulness from the past being extended to the present and indeed into the future. This is a reflection on the great story in which Mary and Elizabeth were caught up and which gave them such energy, passion, and courage. And it begins with Mary:

> My soul magnifies the LORD,
>> and my spirit rejoices in God my Savior,
> for he has looked with favor on the lowliness of
> his servant.
>> Surely, from now on all generations will call
>> me blessed;

> for the Mighty One has done great things for me,
> and holy is his name. (Lk 1:46b–49)

Mary took much of the message given to her by Gabriel into her soul, into the depths of her being. Gabriel had called her "favored," and she incorporated that into her story. He had told her that her son would sit on the throne of his ancestor David, and from now on all generations would call her "blessed." Gabriel had explained that the power of the Most High would overshadow her. "Mighty One" shares the same root word from which we today derive "dynamo" or "dynamic." The Holy Spirit would come upon her, and the child would be called "holy." In spite of her lack of social status—she's a young woman from a back-country town in a poor and often volatile region—and in spite of recognizing that she is "lowly," she has taken God's promise into her heart and allowed it to shape her story and even her identity.

"Great things" is a poetic phrase of remembrance and praise in some of the Psalms. The phrase was a favorite of the Jewish people of Mary's day to express in song and poetry God's intervention for their salvation—for instance: "You who have done great things, O God, who is like you?" (Ps 71:19b); and, "They forgot God, their Savior, who had done great things in Egypt" (Ps 106:21); and, "Then our mouth was filled with laughter, and our tongue with shouts of joy; then it was said among the nations, 'The LORD has done great things for them.' The LORD has done great things for us, and we rejoiced" (Ps 126:2–3).

As in Psalm 106, "great things" is also language used at a climactic point of the Exodus, which is the definitive event in which God intervened for his people and the story through which they became a nation. When the people had been rescued from Egypt and were about to enter the Promised Land, Moses reminded them of all that had happened and called on them to be faithful now as a people: "He is your praise; he is your God, who has done for you these great and awesome things that your own eyes have seen," and, "For it is your own eyes that have seen every great deed that the LORD did" (Dt 10:21, 11:7).

In some amazing way, like the "great things" that God had done to save and give hope to his people in the past—rescue them from slavery, shepherd them through a long and dangerous journey, give them a wonderful home flowing with milk and honey, mature them and wean them away from the idolatry and injustices and excesses of the cultures all around them—Mary's bearing this holy child was another of these same "great things," only concentrated, brought to a tiny, focused point. This "great thing" was applied very personally and specifically to her in order that it may then widen out to the whole of her people and beyond, as we shall now see.

> His mercy is for those who fear him
>   from generation to generation.
> He has shown strength with his arm;
>   he has scattered the proud in the thoughts of their
>   hearts. (Lk 1:50–51)

When God led his people out of slavery and gave them a future and a hope, it was considered a work of mercy done by his "strong right arm," a wonderfully expressive Semitism. It was something so gracious and so full of bountiful gifts that God anticipated the people would become intoxicated, as it were, on the bounty and maybe forget from whence they had come, and how it had all come to be. And so, as they were about to enter the Promised Land, God warned them not to forget. He did so in a poignant passage using the same language and a similar image:

> Because the LORD your God is a merciful God, he will neither abandon you nor destroy you; he will not forget the covenant with your ancestors that he swore to them. For ask now about former ages, long before your own, ever since the day that God created human beings on the earth; ask from one end of heaven to the other: has anything so great as this ever happened or has its like ever been heard of? Has any people ever heard the voice of a god speaking out of a fire, as you have heard, and lived? Or has any god ever attempted to go and take a nation for himself from the midst of another nation, by trials, by signs and wonders, by war, by a mighty hand and an outstretched arm, and by terrifying displays of power, as the LORD your God did for you in Egypt before your very eyes? To

> you it was shown so that you would acknowl-
> edge that the LORD is God; there is no other
> besides him. (Dt 4:31–35)

The great things God did to rescue his people and give them a future and a hope were completely new, unheard of, and jaw-droppingly unexpected. Just as what has happened to Mary, which one day will be seen to effect that same kind of salvation once again, in an even greater manner:

> He has brought down the powerful from their thrones,
>   and lifted up the lowly;
> he has filled the hungry with good things,
>   and sent the rich away empty.
> He has helped his servant Israel,
>   in remembrance of his mercy,
> according to the promise he made to our ancestors,
>   to Abraham and to his descendants forever. (Lk
>   1:52–55)

And so the things that are happening and have brought Mary and Elizabeth together, while unique and unexpected, are not random; they are part of a long and great tapestry that had been on the loom of heaven for many generations, all the way back to God's covenant with and promise to Abraham.

Perhaps this helps to explain the strange past tense of Mary's poem. It seems odd that she would speak as if these things had been accomplished already. Then again, wonders of God had happened before. Since such events renew and move that great story forward, they can also be seen in some sense as prophetically definite, though the completion of these promises would come later—not only for Mary and Elizabeth (births and lives of Jesus and John and the subsequent events recorded in Luke's gospel) but also for us. Advent is, of course, not only a season of remembering God's presence in his great acts of the past, but also a season of looking forward to his renewed perfect presence with us, when Jesus, who has won the victory already though the battle rages on, returns in glory, and we at last see him face-to-face.

Now that we have paused to feel the weight of the moment, Luke can close the scene. This time he gives just a glance to Elizabeth's gestational clock, the timekeeper for the story. He had told us that Gabriel had come to Mary six months into Elizabeth's pregnancy and that Mary had gone "with haste" to see her. Now, "Mary remained with her about three months and then returned to her home" (Lk 1:56). And, again, as a major character moves off the stage, the scene closes.

Our Question

When we entered this scene things had changed: rather than meeting the messenger from heaven we saw people on fire with the joy of having a role in God's great story and energetically acting out their parts. We noticed that when one sees oneself as a part of a great story, it is easier to "keep the plot," no matter what comes along. It's easier to keep moral courage and, when necessary, to sacrifice.

We also saw God use the poor and otherwise lowly—even those who had come to see themselves as defined by suffering and shame—and allow them to slough all that off and find the freedom of forgetting themselves for a while so they could walk in unrestrained, visceral joy.

There were moments during those years in northern Virginia when I found myself asking, "Who am I?" God had given my life a happy reversal, and there I was—even me—aware of my limitations and country upbringing and failures and all the rest, and yet God had given me the incredible privilege of being called to serve in a great story of his great heart for the poor and lowly. Part of my work was to lead followers of Jesus who were from arguably the most powerful city in the world into relationship with our brothers and sisters in faith who are poor or living in the slums of some sprawling city in the two-thirds world or being persecuted for their faith. Those poor or suffering or in danger so often seemed to have a more immediate sense of God's presence and of God as a living hope, even in the face of all in their lives that was not as it should have been.

One of the deep sources of inspiration that I found in those years was a German pastor-theologian who was brilliant, courageous, and able to keep the plot, even in the midst of great turmoil. Dietrich Bonhoeffer was brilliant; he wrote not one but two doctoral dissertations—throwing in an extra one just to answer his own questions, it seems. When Hitler began to take power, Bonhoeffer saw the danger immediately and spoke out clearly. It is a long and complex story, well worth reading but not for us to cover in detail right now; for our purposes it is enough to know that eventually, inevitably, he was too threatening, so international friends advised him to flee. He fled to the United Kingdom and the United States, but his conscience troubled him for taking a relatively easy way out while others of his like-minded countrymen struggled on in danger. So he returned to Germany, against his friends' advice and urgent pleading. He had, through it all, kept the plot. When he got back to Germany, he began an underground seminary. He was caught, arrested, and put in prison camp at Buchenwald. Survivors later related that he was stalwart, an encouragement to the other prisoners, as if a chaplain to them. During that time he also wrote this remarkable poem:

> *Who Am I?*
>
> Who am I? They often tell me
> I stepped from my cell's confinement
> Calmly, cheerfully, firmly,
> Like a squire from his country-house.
> Who am I? They often tell me
> I used to speak to my warders
> Freely and friendly and clearly,
> As though it were mine to command.
> Who am I? They also tell me
> I bore the days of misfortune
> Equally, smilingly, proudly,
> Like one accustomed to win.

Am I then really all that which other men
    tell of?
Or am I only what I myself know of myself?
Restless and longing and sick, like a bird in
    a cage,
Struggling for breath, as though hands were
compressing my throat,
Yearning for colors, for flowers, for the
voices of birds,
Thirsting for words of kindness,
for neighborliness,
Tossing in expectation of great events,
Powerlessly trembling for friends at an
infinite distance,
Weary and empty at praying, at thinking,
at making,
Faint, and ready to say farewell to it all?

Who am I? This or the other?
Am I one person today and
tomorrow another?
Am I both at once? A hypocrite
before others,
And before myself a contemptibly
woebegone weakling?
Or is something within me still like a
beaten army,
Fleeing in disorder from victory
already achieved?

> Who am I? They mock me, these lonely
> questions of mine.
> Whoever I am, Thou knowest, O God,
> I am Thine![3]

There are those in our culture who feel that humility is the province of the unaccomplished and indeed the incapable, but that is not so. And we have been challenged this Advent to risk the belief that God may want to draw near to us and more closely enter our lives—if we have been willing to accept that there is more room for the Spirit to work in the midst of this world than perhaps we had known or wanted to risk believing. Can we take the next step to feeling a sense of wonder that it would be even *us*—you and me—to whom God would want to draw near and use for his purposes? Can we turn the corner from our own sense of past failures and regrets to a place of wonder that our lives might amount to so much more, caught up in heaven's weaving?

The Challenge of the Third Week

This is the challenge for this third week in Advent: to pray the "Magnificat" each evening with so many brothers and sisters around the world and, after we do, to take the step of bringing the areas of shame and regret to the Lord in prayer and giving them up to him. Ask for the grace to see ourselves as his children, with whom he is, and who he chooses to use in his great story. And as we take that step in faith, might we even smile?

On the whole in Luke's story so far, the men are not coming off so well. The scene we have just walked through took us into the world of women: two women who were not only relatives but also dear friends, with lots of (wonderfully) shameless and expressive emotion, and babies on the way. In the next scene, we meet Zechariah again, and we discover whether the men in the story will begin to catch up.

Where Is God *Leading Me?*

The morning that I scheduled to begin to research this chapter had as its first business to meet a friend over coffee. By this time it had been nearly three years since he had been employed. He lost his professional job in a large corporation in his city during the economic downturn of our time, and he and his family had been just holding on ever since. Self-doubt, guilt, a crushing sense of worthlessness, and depression—he has fought valiantly simply to "stay in the game." He's fought to keep getting up day after day, to encourage his wife who has been forced to work overtime, to do things around the house that perhaps do not come naturally to him, and to be a father whose children benefit and find energy and life from his presence rather than being dragged down into the quagmire in which he feels he is stuck.

I believe he has fought well, remarkably well. He has managed to keep his mind sound; he has even managed to keep a sense of perspective. He has taken what piecemeal work he has been able to find. And amazingly, in some sense, he has been able to take the whole period as a sort of spiritual conservatory, a kind of spiritual hothouse, and in it he has grown in the spiritual life, particularly in prayer and in knowledge of the Bible.

On the morning I began to research this chapter, we laughed together in delight. Out of the proverbial blue he had just had two jobs presented to him, one without his looking for it. Neither job was perfect, and neither was something he would have expected to do just a handful of years ago. But either would significantly help his family, and he could see himself doing something worthwhile. The look in his eyes had lightened, and a sense of expectation seemed to hang about him in the air. He believed again that God had remembered him and was moving in his life.

The People's Question

In his last scene before Jesus' birth, Luke reconnects us with a man who was, in a sense, taken out of the normal loop of his public life, and who had been given a period of spiritual gestation, to wait, to ponder, to pray, and perhaps to have his perspective and the ability to believe renewed.

Now Luke will bring us to meet Zechariah again, to see whether the gestation had produced any useful fruit.

But first he checks the clock on the narrative wall, which is Elizabeth's more regular gestation—a child in the womb of a pregnant woman. And all has gone well: "Now the time came for Elizabeth to give birth, and she bore a son" (Lk 1:57). A more literal rendering would indicate that "the time [of her gestation] was *fulfilled*" (italics added). This is the same notion which Gabriel had given to Zechariah back in verse 20: "Because you did not believe my words, which will be fulfilled in their time, you will become mute, unable to speak, until the day these things occur."

And then we are reminded that all of this, though normal and natural, was originally a plan from beyond the veil, in heaven, as the next verse also confirms: "Her neighbors and relatives heard that the LORD had shown his great mercy to her, and they rejoiced with her" (Lk 1:58).

Having reminded us of this bigger picture, Luke then gives one of his favorite clues that heaven is on the move, and that things beyond the natural are about to happen: he uses that little Greek word which we translate as "and it came about." The New Revised Standard Version translates verse 59 as: "On the eighth day they [her excited neighbors and relatives] came to circumcise the child, and they were going to name him Zechariah after his father" (Lk 1:59). But again, a more literal translation catches Luke's nuance and his brilliance as a storyteller. It might go something like this: "And it came about in the eighth day that they came to circumcise the child, and they were calling him by the name of his father, Zechariah."

In this scene the mob of well-wishing relatives and neighbors takes on one voice, one will; it is as if they act as one character in the narrative. Dare we propose that anyone with a large and well-connected extended family or having grown up in a smallish town is likely to be able to identify with this phenomenon? The relatives and neighbors do not mean any ill; they do not yet know that this is weaving from beyond the veil, so they go on as usual.

Still, Luke has signaled us that something is about to happen, and it is Elizabeth who once again shows herself faithful, standing up to the mob with a bold and direct statement: "But his mother said, 'No; he is to be called John'" (Lk 1:60). Did you notice the subtle shift in the lead-up to her words? As much as Luke is a kind of a romantic story-teller and a friend to the lowly, the poor, women, and the overlooked, he is also a detailed, efficient, and determined reporter. While Elizabeth has been a heroine of faith, now we come to the place such that her part in this great drama, which heaven is working out, moves off center stage. She is now, even just immediately after her son's birth and before he has been named, no longer referred to as Elizabeth; she is now "his mother."

This is not a break in Luke's warm heart for her or those in her situation; she has been and is being portrayed in a very favorable light. In this moment she stands out as a virtual lioness of courage and faith and makes the initial act of faith that connects the plan from heaven with the realities of life on earth. She speaks up and stands against the collected weight of tradition and its conventions, which would be no small thing in her culture and her day.

Still, the point of this strand of heaven's weaving has been to reignite the spirit of prophecy that had so long been silent, and that would rest in and flow from her son. He would in some mysterious and real sense be the long-awaited return of Elijah, who the people believed must prophesy again before the Messiah would come, based on the words of the prophet Malachi: "Lo, I will send you the prophet Elijah before the great and terrible day of the LORD comes. He will turn the hearts of parents to their children and the hearts of children to their parents, so that I will not come and strike the land with a curse" (Mal 4:5–6). And so now that John is about to be circumcised, which is to say he is about to be marked by the cutting that brings him into the covenant of his people, Luke deftly moves the wee infant to the narrative forefront. And his mother, lioness though she is, he gently moves a step or two toward exiting stage right.

It is very nearly the same for his father. The mob is surprised or maybe even a bit indignant with Elizabeth's direct statement, and "they said to her, 'None of your relatives has this name'" (Lk 1:61). We should not be surprised to see them try to take matters into their own hands: "Then they began motioning to his father to find out what name he wanted to give him" (Lk 1:62). "His father." Even the priest who was the first character we met in Luke's reporting is now being subordinated to the first miracle baby, because the plan of God which is so tantalizingly being woven into life controls and comes to the forefront.

So the dramatic tension rises. We have not interacted with Zechariah since he was sent for a "time out" way back in the first scene of Luke's great story. What has come of his gestational silence and the solitude that would naturally have accompanied it? Has his heart mended? Is his faith deeply restored? Will a man (at last) show himself well in the story?

"He asked for a writing tablet and wrote, 'His name is John.' And all of them were amazed. Immediately his mouth was opened and his tongue freed, and he began to speak, praising God" (Lk 1:63–64). The word order in the Greek for those all-important words of Zechariah is actually "John is his name." This is something to notice because it puts the shocking confirmation right up there at the front.

Up to this point the mob had rejoiced, and now they are amazed. Zechariah, for his part, has spent his gestational silence and the ensuing solitude well and affirms a plan put in action beyond convention: the weaving. God is at work, and the people are beginning to notice and will all the more, given what happens next: "Immediately his mouth was opened and his tongue freed, and he began to speak, praising God" (Lk 1:64). Gabriel's judgment, which he had put upon Zechariah not for ill but rather for healing, has taken its course and had its desired effect. Zechariah is freed, not only to speak again, but also to believe again, to hope again, to savor the passing days of life again, and to rejoice again. And so he blesses God.

"And fear came to be on all those living near and in the whole of the hill country of Judea all these things were discussed" (Lk 1:65, AT). It is a warm, dynamic scene—humble people in regular homes all across the region stirred as anticipation reverberates among them so strongly that "all who heard these things put them in their hearts, saying, 'What then will this child be?' for the hand of the LORD was with him" (Lk 1:66, AT). Luke is masterful in relaying the human element; the people are touched to their core, as well they might be, for God is indeed doing something special and rare.

"The hand of the LORD" is a powerful image in the Old Testament, a vivid way of imagining God reaching into the affairs of life. Most often the phrase is connected with judgment, and strong judgment, the sort that comes only after God has waited long and suffered his patience long being tried. But the phrase is not always connected that way. On one poignant occasion when David had disobeyed the Lord, he was confronted by the seer Gad with the hard choice: natural disaster, or a period of the triumph of his enemies, or a time of God's judgment. David chose the third option saying, "Let me fall into the hand of the LORD, for his mercy is very great; but let me not fall into human hands" (1 Chr 21:13).

And there are rare but wonderful moments in the Old Testament when "the hand of the LORD" acts to lend God's agent power for some unique and critical act of rescue or redemption. Elijah, when he had defeated the prophets of Baal in the spiritual power showdown on Mount Carmel, rather than having time to savor the victory, found himself in the gravest danger he had yet faced. For now Elijah had attracted the deadly attention, not only of Ahab, but also of Jezebel; and Jezebel was the link tying Israel to the regional empire of the Sidonians, an empire of unscrupulous expediency. Thus he hurried along beyond normal human ability because "the hand of the LORD was on Elijah; he girded up his loins and ran in front of Ahab to the entrance of Jezreel" (1 Kgs 18:46).

And in another moment, Ezra and his people had been exiled to Persia, but then Artaxerxes, King of Persia, had given him permission to go back to Jerusalem to begin to rebuild. When he had been granted not only permission but also a mandate of the king to begin what he longed to do (knowing it was a daunting and indeed extremely dangerous task), Ezra was able to rise to the challenges. He did so because he understood himself to be playing out the role God had especially given for his very life. So he "took courage, for the hand of the LORD my God was upon me, and I gathered leaders from Israel to go up with me" (Ezr 7:28).

And one last beautiful example of the enabling power for redemption of the "hand of the LORD" occurred when Ezekiel was given the powerful vision of the resurrection to come. It was the vision of a valley of dry bones coming back to embodied life: "The hand of the LORD came upon me, and he brought me out by the spirit of the LORD and set me down in the middle of a valley; it was full of bones" (Ez 37:1).

Both senses of the phrase are well suited to John the Baptist. We see at the end of this scene that "the child grew and became strong in spirit, and he was in the wilderness until the day he appeared publicly to Israel" (Lk 1:80). He was filled with the Holy Spirit since before his birth, and God would continue to be near to him and to strengthen him for the unique and difficult job he was to accomplish. But the judgment aspect is suited to the story as well, for John's message would be one of repentance; he would be an agent of declaring that judgment was coming if people did not get ready for the coming of the Lord. Judgment and good news exist simultaneously: prepare for the grace and great love and new life that are near.

And so the effect of the hand of the Lord upon this child was felt throughout the region, and reverberated through hearts and recurred in the conversations of the people, leading them to ask in anticipation, "What then will this child be?" Luke has so far told us a story that has focused around two unexpected (gestational) expectations. Now that one of those expectations has been fulfilled the dramatic tension is not lessened but ironically is intensified in awaiting the second birth. It "sits in the air," to borrow Shakespeare's phrase. God was showing mercy to one of his beloved daughters, and that was only the beginning. It was a joyful way to weave the actors into the dramatic mission to come.

The people sensed that God was at work in a special way and wondered where it all would go. How far ranging was the plan of heaven, which had begun in these wonders they had seen or about which they had heard? Their question, like the three that precede it, primarily exists as a part of Luke's narrative of sharing the wondrous happenings that came at that time, the beginning of the most defining events in all of history. But like the other three questions, this question can reach up off the page and out of its historical moment to enter our imaginations and draw our hearts in. The question may be transferable to us, even as it maintains its own original and primary integrity.

Our Question

"What then will this child be?" If we let this question speak to us in both ways then it is for us the fourth question of our Advent spiritual journey. The first question challenged us to wrestle with our disappointments and frustrations and sit with God in silence, waiting upon the renewal and healing of our hearts. The second question challenged us to open up to there being more space in the midst of life where God could work, even in ways beyond what we may be able to understand. The third question pushed into deeper space in our hearts: we were challenged to move beyond abstract possibilities and ponder whether God might truly love *even me* and choose to act in and through me for the glory of his name and the benefit of his kingdom.

These are not easy questions. They should have pushed us out of our comfort zones, breaking up whatever "settling" we've done with life and the limits we feel we've found on reality. They should have challenged the compromises we've struck with God and the universe in order that we might reduce disappointment and feel less pain. Now we've begun to open up again, and so the question of these robust, simple hill people perhaps can become our new perspective as well. Perhaps the universe no longer is a closed system; perhaps it is an open-ended relationship in which we begin to wonder, "How much is possible, especially when we live in the presence of God?"

And this is an appropriate Advent attitude. In Advent we prepare to celebrate the historical, personal, and incarnate presence of God weaving himself into history in a humble and vulnerable form as a babe. The baby would grow up to be a strong man and a very strong man at that, but nevertheless just one life pitted against everything evil could throw at him. In those challenges, count his family being displaced by ethnic strife when he was an infant, and add challenges all the way through his life of struggles and conflict until at last the empire and his own people conspired together to be rid of him—and that by public torture and shame. In Advent we prepare to celebrate that beautiful, heartrending love, which would visit us in humility and suffer so; but in Advent we also look ahead to Jesus' future return in glory and power, the great King coming to reign, and we wonder what it will be to behold such glory. What will it be when God's presence is once more all in all, covering all as the waters cover the seas?

And yet along with those two movements of looking back and looking forward, in Advent we also wait in the present for a renewed sense of God's presence with us now in spite of and in the midst of "whatever." And so our challenge in these last days of Advent, as we draw near to the birth of Christ and Christmas Day, is to wait with an open spirit, open to a different future, a brighter one, even in our own lives and before that ultimate fulfillment of Jesus' return. But this is a hope we do not hold tightly. It is one that we rather hold in trust, aware that we do not know what path things may take and how far they may go; but also we are confident that we go to meet them not alone but with the presence of our God. But it sometimes seems as if God enjoys things more as an adventure than as a predictable journey. And so there is an anticipation that tingles, in part for defying our efforts to contain it, and that is okay because of the base of trust that has been building and the experience of God's presence.

But for all that we cannot know, perhaps on the other hand we can name areas of life where God has been at work during this Advent season. And in those areas we are excitedly waiting to see "what will all this be?" And there are at least clues that give us a sense of where God's works have gone in the past and what is in keeping with who God is and what he cares about. One of the best expressions of these clues comes in the pause in Luke's gospel at this important moment for the second poetic reflection, the second canticle. This canticle acts as an answer to the question that is open on the table—the people's question: "What will this be?" or, as the southern country folks around whom I grew up would say, "What all is God up to in all of this?"

The Canticle of Zechariah

Zechariah has come full circle; while it is true that he has already redeemed himself, so to speak, and his voice has been restored, now we get a glimpse of the depth of the renewal that he has experienced. He catches up with his wife and his infant son who have already been filled with the Holy Spirit, and he completes the circuit for his little family as he too is filled: "And Zechariah, his father, was filled with the Holy Spirit and prophesied" (Lk 1:67, AT).

What he spoke was inspired, and like the first canticle, the "Magnificat," Zechariah's canticle has taken its place in worship over the centuries and is known by its first Latin word as the "Benedictus." It is the canticle particular to Morning Prayer in the churches of the West. And the "Benedictus," like the "Magnificat," is dense and debated in terms of its poetic form; it does not help that in the grammar of the original Greek the whole of its twelve verses form but one sentence. But as with the "Magnificat," we will not linger over the complexities but will try to catch the point. The happy news is that the pointers to God's character and his actions ring clear. As perhaps one might expect from the words of a priest of the Jewish people, the "Benedictus" is so full of Old Testament allusions and references to God's promises and praises that it has been described by some as a mosaic.[1]

The "Benedictus" begins with introductory praise to God: "Blessed be the LORD, the God of Israel" (Lk 1:68a,

AT). Immediately the mind of the priest is evident, for in the Psalms this phrase transitions into the ending part of three of the five sections (or books) into which the larger Book of Psalms has traditionally been divided:[2]

> Blessed be the LORD, the God of Israel,
> from everlasting to everlasting.
>> Amen and Amen. (Ps 41:13)
>
> Blessed be the LORD, the God of Israel,
>> who alone does wondrous things. (Ps 72:18)
>
> Blessed be the LORD, the God of Israel,
>> from everlasting to everlasting.
> And let all the people say, "Amen."
>> Praise the LORD! (Ps 106:48)

The "Benedictus" begins in this same way and continues along a similar path—it gives glory to God for his faithfulness and his mighty acts to save his people:

> Blessed be the LORD, the God of Israel
> because he has visited and worked redemption for his people,
>> and has raised up a horn of salvation for us
>> in the house of his servant David,
> just as he spoke through the mouth of his holy prophets from ages ago,
> salvation from our enemies and from the hand of all those who hate us. (Lk 1:68–71 AT)

Three strong verbs in the grammar of the Greek state the reasons God is to be blessed: he has "visited," "worked redemption," and "raised up" a way of salvation. Zechariah experienced something of a visit of God through Gabriel, God's messenger, who promised that God's Spirit would work through the son that would come. Zechariah has now had his time in gestational silence to reflect on that visit, and he sees what God is doing with a new and sharpened eye.

What seems odd is that Zechariah also speaks of these things in the *past* tense (as Mary had in the "Magnificat")— God *has visited*, *has worked*, and *has raised up*. It is a paradox: on the one hand, what has happened up to this point is so little compared to what needs to be done; but on the other hand, what has happened is so far beyond what was expected and where life was for Zechariah less than one year ago. What Zechariah believes is happening is momentous, a major turn, as the rest of his canticle will show. So he might be forgiven for speaking proleptically; his renewed eyes of faith understand the effect of God's weaving. The situation is perhaps not unlike that old preacher's illustration, which is timeworn and probably overdone but still poignant: on D-day soldiers established beachheads. Though there was much still to do, much courage needed, and much suffering to endure, from another point of view one could say that from that point the victory had been won.

The births of John the Baptist and then especially of Jesus are like that in a way, and the third strong verb echoes this bold confidence. It is attached to a powerful image often pertaining to the house of David, through which God had promised a great house, a great king, a great reign of one who would protect his people and make their way into a bright future. In that house God has "raised up a horn of salvation." A horn is the presenting tool of force on a great and vigorous beast, such as an ox or a bull; and in the Psalms and other Old Testament poetic passages, a horn refers to the pride, the glory, and the strength of a person (especially when that strength is given by and found in God or in his Messiah, his anointed of the house of David). It is a broad image, and there are many illustrations, but a few will bring the image to sharper relief:

> The LORD is my rock, my fortress, and my deliverer,
>   my God, my rock in whom I take refuge,
>   my shield, and the horn of my salvation, my
>   stronghold. (Ps 18:2)

> I will cause a horn to sprout up for David;
> I have prepared a lamp for my anointed one. (Ps 132:17)

In 1 Samuel 2:10, in Hannah's song, the image occurs in the midst of another poetic reflection that comes in the pause of an ongoing narrative: "He will give strength to his king, and exalt the power [horn] of his anointed."

It is such a wide and evocative image. In another excerpt, notice the many points that resonate with the "Benedictus"—the "hand of enemies," for example:

> David spoke to the LORD the words of this
> song on the day when the LORD delivered him
> from the hand of all his enemies, and from
> the hand of Saul. He said:
> The LORD is my rock, my fortress,
> and my deliverer,
> my God, my rock, in whom I take refuge,
> my shield and the horn of my salvation.
> (2 Sam 22:1–3)

So the powerful image of the "horn of salvation" brings
the mind to reflect on the Messiah as victorious warrior,
strong as a bull or an ox, anointed and chosen of the house
of David, the king and patriarch of his royal house. And
then in the next verses, Zechariah recalls that this hope
has been before them for a long time. The inspiring Spirit
of God consistently presented hope to them. Even when
speaking through various prophets in different times, it
was the (singular) "mouth" of the (plural) "holy prophets
of long ago."

This hope has what we might call an official aspect
because it is looking to a royal house, a reign, and a king.
Thus it would be corporate in its effect: "salvation from our
enemies and from the hand of all those who hate us." As
we have seen, "the hand of the LORD" was often an image
of God's judgment; so "the hand of enemies" would refer
to the military might of the kingdoms of the world of their
day, who had for so long oppressed them. And there had
been plenty: Assyrians, Babylonians, Greeks, Seleucids, or
in Zechariah's time, Romans.

Perhaps it seems here that Zechariah has rocketed beyond mere renewal of his own faith and flown off beyond reason! One might say his claim seemed impossible, and truth be told it would be a long time indeed and enigmatically done before the "leaven" of the Gospel would conquer the Romans.[3] But then, his people's story had never been the sure thing. After all, it had all begun when God made a personal, intimate, and seemingly audacious promise of his presence and blessing forever to a wandering nomad. And that nomad, Abraham, had taken it seriously and had arranged his entire life and fate around it. And this made the way possible for a new people to come into being.

As Zechariah's poem continues, he reaches back to this foundation stone: God is to be blessed because he has promised a ruler Messiah for the house of David and also because of the personal, intimate promise he made with Abraham that meant that God was determined:

> To work mercy for our fathers
> and to remember his holy covenant,
> The oath that he swore to Abraham
> our father,
> To grant to us that we, without fear of our
> enemies, be delivered
> To worship him in holiness and righteousness
> before him all our days. (Lk 1:72–75, AT)[4]

To "work mercy" is a term from the Old Testament used to express God's long-suffering faithfulness; God is one who shows "steadfast love to the thousandth generation of those who love me and keep my commandments," as is proclaimed twice in Exodus (20:6 and similarly in 34:7) and is restated for effect in Deuteronomy (5:10). In the Old Testament, this mercy comes to effect when God "remembers" one who was in hardship or danger. For that person this represents the great moment of hope; at that point God would intervene to save. God "remembered" Noah who was stuck in the ark, and the waters of the flood began to dry; and then God gave the rainbow, and he promised upon seeing it to "remember the everlasting covenant between God and every living creature of all flesh that is on the earth" (Gn 8:1, 9:16).

He "remembered" Rachel who, like Elizabeth, had been barren; and he granted her a son (Gn 30:22). He "remembered" Abraham and for his sake rescued Lot from Sodom and Gomorrah (Gn 19:29). And supremely when the people of Israel were enslaved in Egypt under the thumb of the empire of their time, "God heard their groaning, and God remembered his covenant with Abraham, Isaac, and Jacob," (Ex 2:24) and said, "I have also heard the groaning of the Israelites whom the Egyptians are holding as slaves, and I have remembered my covenant" (Ex 6:5).

Zechariah saw God, who was now working mercy afresh and remembering his covenant, making a way for the people to begin again to have the kind of intimate, dynamic, *living* relationship that Abraham had known. It was the sort of relationship of life-changing faith that had been so crucial to their whole story's beginning. That renewal would begin with the son—Zechariah's miracle son—who would make the way for the Anointed One, the Messiah.

Abraham had made (an eventual) way for David and his house. In a much more direct way John would make a way for Jesus, as Zechariah sees and predicts:

> And yet even you, child, will be called the prophet of the Most High;
> For you will go before the LORD to prepare his ways,
> to give knowledge of salvation to his people by the forgiveness of their sins. (Lk 1:76–77, AT)[4]

It had been a long wait for the renewal of the prophetic voice, a long wait and a long path of wondering where God was and what was going on beyond the veil. Zechariah now shows the full strength of his own personal renewal—he believes in the weaving from beyond the veil so strongly now that he sees in it the renewal of the prophetic voice. Indeed in this very moment in his poem, he is himself a kind of forerunner to the forerunner, even as he is also father to the son.

And, of course, the renewal of the prophetic voice brings renewal of covenant so that the promise and the relationship it recalls passes from being some kind of historical, ethnic, or cultural memory to being a living relationship on fire again. This is the knowledge of salvation, for to know and be in and with God is to be saved, to live forever with the source, goal, and very definer of life itself. And that salvation is accomplished through the forgiveness of sins—or "release from sins" as it could legitimately be translated—for God is perfectly holy, and we simply are not; but what a relief, what a freedom, to be released, set free, and made clean.

Somewhere in this is the mystery of the deep transformation at the core of individual human beings that would begin as this story went forward; this freedom would transform people and, combined with the hope of the Resurrection, make them love struck in the present and fearless regarding the future. It is difficult to defeat a people who fear nothing and hope for everything; and the early Christians were not defeated, in spite of the overwhelming odds against them. They were the next installment (after only Jesus himself) of that tiny "mustard seed" that would grow over the years to be a great tree in which the birds of the air would come and rest. This itself is an image of a great kingdom with a far reach. And to know this freedom and cleanness is a delight; it allows intoxication on life in the present moment. But we have gotten way ahead of the story. Zechariah reflects that his son will make the way and will bring covenant renewal. The message is a joy for all ages, and to find Zechariah so recovered and robust is a kind of a salve for weary souls.

As the canticle draws to a close it goes full circle and returns to the place where it began: with the promise of

God's visit to establish a royal house of David with a great king to rule forever. That one was coming soon, and the story would go something like this:

> Because of the visceral mercy of our God,
> in which the dawn from on high will visit us,
> to shine on those sitting in darkness and the
> shadow of death,
> to guide our feet in the way of peace. (Lk
> 1:78–79, AT)

I am not an expert in biblical Greek, though I enjoy it; but I will take the risk here of translating as "visceral mercy" what normally gets translated as something like "tender mercy." The adjective in Greek is onomatopoetic; it might be transliterated as *splaghna*, and when one tries to say that in English, one catches the guttural, visceral sense of the word. The *splaghna* were considered the upper inner parts of the body—the heart, the lungs, and the liver—and as such were the seat of the emotions.[5] The word shows up at poignant moments in the gospels, such as the moment when Jesus or a character in one of his parables is deeply moved with compassion—for instance, when the Good Samaritan finds the man beaten, naked, and barely alive by the side of the road. Some versions translate that the Samaritan was "moved with pity." From the point of view of God looking upon us with mercy, *splaghna* is wonderfully good news; it shows the softness, yes, the tenderness, of God's love for his people and their (and our) sufferings. Zechariah's heart is no longer hardened and cynical! Now he believes that God's love for his suffering people is deep, effective, and visceral.

The next line, "in which the dawn from on high will visit us," seems a little stiff, but I made it more literal to bring attention to the recurrence of the word from the beginning of the canticle—God's *visit*. In the earlier part of the canticle what was being raised up was a horn of salvation; now it is "the dawn (or sunrise) from on high," which is another image for the Messiah. This image was current in Jewish expectation, and Greek-speaking Jews of the time are believed to have used it to describe the expected king of the house of David.[6]

Having completed the circle, as it were, the canticle ends with a kind of a flourish: this deep compassion and this bright, new One are coming "to shine on those sitting in darkness and the shadow of death." The second bit is the same phrase made dear to so many hearts from Psalm 23, offering comfort in the hardest times and reflecting the gentler side of the Messiah as shepherd. Ultimately it all comes together "to guide our feet in the way of peace."

Zechariah is recovered, and the people's question is answered, at least prophetically and with powerful images that both look back to God's faithfulness in Israel's history and look forward to the great things he is weaving now.

We have noted that Luke liked to end these scenes by having a character depart. In this case he does that and then some—he speeds up time, as it were, hurrying John the Baptist out into the wilderness: "The child grew and became strong in spirit, and he was in the wilderness until the day of his showing himself to Israel" (Lk 1:80). The time of questions is (temporarily) suspended, to return when Jesus is on stage and active—but still maybe it is better to say that the questions that needed to be asked before Jesus' birth, in Advent, before Christmas, have now been put on the table and into our hearts. They have brought us into the story or have brought the story out to meet us. What come next are two canticles of celebration but without questions to precede them, because God has visited his people and worked redemption for us.

The Challenge of the Fourth Week

My friend, with whom I had coffee just as I began to work on this chapter, worked hard to stay sane over a long period without work. I sat and talked and prayed with him on occasion, but mostly I felt ineffective, nothing like a horn of God's salvation—which, indeed, I was not—but still God remembered him, and things changed, and now he looks at a brighter future. In the time between that day and this, I heard from another old friend in another country with similar glad tidings after two years of struggle to find meaningful work. We talked via an Internet-based video-phone service, and still the relief, the joy, and the anticipation were palpable. Now he felt again that he had a reason to get up in the morning and could wonder where it all could go. He could wonder what God might be doing in all of this that had come to pass so quickly and unexpectedly.

Our challenge as we draw near to Christmas Day is to let our hearts ask that as well—how much will God do in our new futures?

Rejoice in the Romance

When our girls were little, my grandmother gave them a James Herriot book for children. The book was lovely and included a handful of the most touching stories, beautifully illustrated. As I began to read it to them, it became impossible to tell who enjoyed it more, the girls or I. It reintroduced me to that affable, English country veterinarian working the farms of the Yorkshire dales in postwar England and rekindled my love for his stories that began when I had read *All Creatures Great and Small*.

The stories about the little dog Tricky Woo alone are enough to delight and lift the spirits. Tricky Woo is the pampered Pekingese belonging to the matron of the area where Herriot lives. She often calls on Herriot to come visit the manor house and tend to Tricky's mostly imagined ailments, but Herriot does not mind. He quietly coordinates visits around the hour for afternoon sherry and in his good-natured cordiality enjoys conversation with the matron after each treatment. Add to that the gift basket Tricky sent him at Christmas, the thank-you the vet sent back addressed to Master Tricky, and so on, and there is plenty there to make the man's reputation—perhaps not so much as a veterinarian but certainly as one with a keen eye for the human element and for the narrative or "story" quality of it all, for lack of a better way to put it.

But it wasn't only the eccentricities that Herriot could turn into stirring scenes; it was paying visits to piggeries, birthing calves, chasing escaped lambs, or dealing gingerly with angry bulls. In other words, probably pretty much every country veterinarian in mid-twentieth-century England had similar experiences, but only Herriot had the lens to see the life in and behind it all, combined with the wit to tell it in an endearing manner. His storytelling did not offer people hope or self-help advice on the power of joy. Rather, it simply exuded hope and joy, and so people flocked to it to feed their souls.

During those days that I was rediscovering James Herriot, it occurred to me that though my pastoral work has not typically been cloak-and-dagger, full of clandestine conspiratorial secrets, especially dangerous, or history-shifting, still it was like Herriot's veterinary work in that the stuff of life is there—get involved with living people and God's whole good creation and there is humor, irony, joy, pathos, and often surprise. Sometimes, yes, it has been remarkably dramatic—whether happy or sad—and amazingly unexpected. It is miraculous to sense the intervention of the Spirit of God in a heightened manner working with the otherwise unexplainable. But most of the time it is "just" the regular miraculous reality of the gift of life continuing; it's good and wonderful and to be appreciated, yet it is somewhat mundane and regular. A trick to joy is to not turn the lenses of wonder off during these periods of the predictable. Some have suggested that perhaps it works this way rather than the other way around—if one can keep the lenses of wonder during the mundane, then one can see the wildly, uniquely miraculous when it happens; if the wonder dries up, the more likely the miraculous is missed though it be right before the eyes.

A Living Story

Perhaps it is for these sorts of reasons that Luke was chosen by the Spirit of God to be one of the four evangelists. Tradition holds that he was a doctor, and certainly he had a strong sense of pastoral presence and of sympathetic imagination. He had the keen eye for the human element and the story in each life, whether anonymous and predictable or grand and exceptional. He had the lenses to see the wonder and worth of life in the everyday and the heart to see the overtly miraculous when it came.

Of all the evangelists, Luke best tells the Christmas story, catching the romantic ethos that is due it. I can still remember my boyhood amazement at a dear elderly and pious woman in my church. The woman had been confined to a wheelchair for as long as I had known her, and each year on Christmas Eve she would be wheeled by her gentle husband to the front of the church and would recite from memory Luke's Christmas story. It sent shivers up and down my spine, every year.

And so we approach the romantic climax, the Messiah's birth. Luke has been painting a picture for us of weavings orchestrated from heaven; and though the Word exists as an eternal thread before and beyond all of life, nonetheless for a while he wove himself from beyond the veil into life in this dimension. Luke has taken care to show the beginning moves and follow the strands that come together. He has told all with sympathy, pathos, joy, and with a lens that can see the big picture while still keeping a warm heart for the particular, and he has led us along a journey as he went.

We saw the couple, Zechariah and Elizabeth, who were pious, humble, faithful, and beautiful souls but for whom life had not been easy. And "it came about" that Zechariah got chosen by lot, or so he thought; but Luke had the sense to see that the lot was loaded because God wanted to pull Zechariah into a place apart for a consultation with Gabriel. And, amazing love, it was not only in order to begin the weaving but also to bring about renewal for Zechariah.

God works a sort of spiritual multivariable calculus, and it is beautiful.

Luke then took us farther down into the mundane, from a priest before the people on the biggest day of his career to a woman unknown, living in a remote place, without power or prestige or anything seemingly remarkable. Yet Gabriel came to her as well, and gave her a message that was deeply invasive and would completely rearrange her life and expectations. She believed and made herself available: "Let it be done unto me according to your word."

We were brought then to a remarkable scene, especially for that time and for a story set in the ancient Near East: a scene among women. In Luke's telling of the attitudes and actions of women he shows respect for them and their ways. The women are shown seeing and believing at a level where as yet the men feared to tread. Could God use even people such as these, considered not fully human in so many cultures of their times?

And then things really began to move; the first birth came and the joyful first fruits of renewal. Zechariah recovered his heart and faith to the point of being extremely bold, and his voice was restored as well. The people began to notice as the weaving began to show—the gilded threads were impossible to hide for too long—and to wonder and ponder about where those threads came from. And how beautiful would the tapestry of life become now? The talk and the energy began to spread among the hills and the common folk.

Now the questions have been asked and the anticipated moment has come. Luke, the genius storyteller with the ability to see the moment (from the big-picture political all the way down to the individual and personal), will shine as he brings it all together. And this time as we walk through what he has given us, our pace will be a little different because Luke writes two tight paragraphs that cover the necessary ground very quickly. The issue that is piqued at the top of the first paragraph is resolved at the bottom of the second. We will comment as we go, but our main trick is to hold the overall picture of the two paragraphs together and keep them both in view.

Luke's first step in the first paragraph is with one deft stroke to reset the story from a wide-angle perspective, against the backdrop of the social and political realities of his time, and then to narrow the focus to a regional governor, a particular town, and the holy couple in their distress:[1]

> It came about in those days that there went out a decree from Caesar Augustus that all the world should be registered. This was the first registration that came about when Quirinius was governor of Syria. And all went to be registered, each to his own town. And so Joseph went up from Galilee, from the town of Nazareth, into Judea into the town of David that is called Bethlehem, because he was from the house and lineage of David. He went to be registered with Mary, who was

> engaged to him, and who was expecting a
> child. (Lk 2:1–5, AT)

By this point we should not be surprised to meet the phrase "it came about," leading into this new scene. We have seen that it is one of Luke's favorites. It hints that what is happening on earth is not the whole story, and that what meets our eye may in fact be the result of planning and orchestration from the heavens. If ever there were a time to employ that concept, it would seem that time is now and continues on up to the moment the Messiah is born.

But how does that show here? We see the common people scurry about because the empire says so; the empire needs knowledge for control, and the Romans did quite a bit of census taking, the historians tell us. It is a part of how one keeps subjugated peoples subjugated: even the mere act of taking a census reminds them implicitly who is in charge. Agents of the empire pass from village to village, door to door. Sometimes people have to pick up and take on the hassle and expense of interrupting normal life to travel. The lives of the ordinary people are fodder for the machine, and as yet we do not see the irony behind the hubris. Luke will show it to us, but first he continues:

> And it came about as they were there that
> the days were fulfilled for her to give birth,
> and she gave birth to her firstborn son and
> wrapped him in cloths and laid him in a
> manger because there was no room for them
> in the inn. (Lk 2:6–7, AT)

It is remarkable, really. This greatest moment in history is delivered with such brevity and seeming economy of flourish. Luke is not a modern blogger. He does not overuse the exclamation point. Once again Luke uses one of his favorite terms; it gives nuance, a hint, but Luke is loading it up in these few verses—the heavens are up to something. So far all we can really deduce is that even the Messiah seems caught in the empire's web of control. Even when he is in the womb, his nascent life is made difficult; and therefore his identifying with our dirt, pain, tiredness, with our constant battle against the hassles and necessities of life, has already begun. God incarnate knows our suffering indeed.

But still there's some larger point Luke is working toward, and when the story takes an unexpected turn we begin to see. We'll take it a little more literally than it usually gets translated, and perhaps we'll pick up a little of the color of the way Luke tells stories:

> There were shepherds in that area who were outdoors watching their watch over their flocks at night. And an angel of the LORD appeared to them and the glory of the LORD shone on them and they feared a great fear. And the angel said to them: "Do not fear, for behold I proclaim good news to you, a great joy which will be to all the people, because this day is born to you in the city of David a savior, which is Christ, the LORD. And this

> is a sign to you, you will find the newborn
> baby wrapped in cloths and lying in a man-
> ger." And suddenly there came about with the
> angel a multitudinous army of heaven, prais-
> ing God and saying:
>
>> Glory to God in the highest
>> and on earth peace to the people he favors. (Lk
>> 2:8–14, AT)

If this were a play by Shakespeare, at the appearance
of the shepherds one would think that we had left the main
narrative for a scene of comic relief. In modern times we
have romanticized shepherds and imagined their lives idyllic. Perhaps no one has painted that sentiment lovelier than
has Christopher Marlowe, a contemporary of Shakespeare.
In his poem, "The Passionate Shepherd to His Love," the
shepherd appeals to the one he loves that she come share a
simple but bucolic peasant's life with him. The first verse
gives the sense:

> Come live with me and be my love,
> And we will all the pleasures prove
> That valleys, groves, hills, and fields,
> Woods, or steepy mountain yields.[2]

It is a great poem and works well for Valentine's Day; but,
alas, all that we know of a shepherd's life in the ancient
Near East would tend to make the idyllic, romantic view
unlikely. In that time shepherding was more the province
of the lowly—those on the outs and forced to take the last
possibility open for work. In that part of the world in those

ancient days, the job was dangerous. The habitat for the bear and the lion overlapped, for instance. In our day it would be rare to find oneself someplace where one has to beware of one or the other, and to risk meeting both in the wild would take some creative camping indeed.

So we don't realize how strange this turn in the story would have been to an original reader. Why would Luke include a bit about shepherds? Why would he dignify them in such an important moment? They are not the sorts one would think to call upon to validate the story one was telling. Clearly this means that their appearance is important, or it would not be there. This is the way the Bible often works, especially given the brilliance of a writer like Luke.

To be fair I should say that as far as I know, no one really is sure why it is that the shepherds show up right here; one is tempted to suggest that it is because Jesus would, of course, call himself the Good Shepherd, but that is not in Luke's gospel. But one intriguing observation does come to mind; their very lowliness means they may be some of the few who are essentially outside the empire's machinations, just precisely for being so lowly. They sit, as it were, on the edge of society and perhaps are not intertwined enough to be worth the bother. But maybe for all that they are freer than most. Who knows? At any rate the shepherds are not scurrying off to make Rome happy—they are out in the fields by night presumably doing pretty much what they do every night. So maybe the romanticizing of them has the proverbial grain of truth: the world has its concerns but these lowly ones are at rest—at least until the shock comes.

The Song of the Angels

And then an angel, a messenger from heaven, is back on stage; and Luke is completing the circle, tying up the loose ends from the beginning of this scene, when he hinted that heaven was behind it all. A window from heaven is opened, and we hear it directly, and well we might, for it is poignant: "Behold I proclaim good news to you, a great joy which will be to all the people, because this day is born to you in the city of David a savior, which is Christ, the Lord" (Lk 2:10–11, AT). One wouldn't think from the way we tend to picture angels that they would have any sharp and contrary directness about them, but when it is needed, apparently they do. And though it was not apparently clear to us in this instance, it was needed.

Luke has located all of this over and against Caesar Augustus. When Augustus began to reign, he quelled competing claims for the Roman throne and hence was credited with bringing peace to the world. In his honor a great altar to peace was set up a handful of years before this night; the Greek cities of Asia Minor adopted his birthday as the first day of the new year; an inscription at Halicarnassus called him "savior of the whole world." An inscription found in Priene claimed about Augustus that "the birthday of the god has marked the beginning of the good news for the world."[3]

And so the "god" Augustus speaks, and the common people scurry about; but Luke lets his readers hear the angel in order that they (we) realize that even the presumptuous machinations of the empire, though they in their turn will be judged, can in the meantime be turned by God to his own purposes. They are merely working the beater, beam, and treadles of God's loom, unaware.

The politically subversive sense of this moment has largely been lost on us, but it would not have been on Luke's original audience. The angel's words to the shepherds are of the same genre as those proclamations about Augustus: they too are the proclamation of a new king born on "this day"—another little phrase hinting that what is happening in history reflects the pleasure of eternity in heaven.[4] The great prophecy of Isaiah 9 comes to mind, and maybe that chorus of Handel's *Messiah* might echo in your head as well:

> For a child has been born for us,
>> a son given to us;
> authority rests upon his shoulders;
>> and he is named
> Wonderful Counsellor, Mighty God,
>> Everlasting Father, Prince of Peace.
> His authority shall grow continually,
>> and there shall be endless peace
> for the throne of David and his kingdom.
>> He will establish and uphold it
> with justice and with righteousness
>> from this time onwards and for evermore.
> The zeal of the Lord of hosts will do this.
> (Isaiah 9:6–7)

And it is Micah's prophesy as well that reveals the real power that is moving things about to make the way for the true king:

> But you, O Bethlehem of Ephrathah,
>> who are one of the little clans of Judah,
> from you shall come forth for me
>> one who is to rule in Israel,
> whose origin is from of old,
>> from ancient days.
> Therefore he shall give them up until the time
>> when she who is in labor has brought forth;
> then the rest of his kindred shall return
>> to the people of Israel.
> And he shall stand and feed his flock in the strength
> of the LORD,
>> in the majesty of the name of the LORD his God.
> And they shall live secure, for now he shall be great
>> to the ends of the earth;
>> and he shall be the one of peace. (Mi 5:2–5a)

It has been a long time in coming, but it had been planned from before time, and it has come at just the right time. It is touching that the heavens open and the angel choir sings, for from one perspective all that is now in motion means only lowering, pain, humility, and even humiliation for the king of heaven. Indeed, all of that has already begun. And yet there is an overflow from heaven and a great choir appears. Why? For love and honor, I suppose. God is on the earth, and God will be praised. At times it seems not so much an imperative as an inevitability, an inherent reality in the very DNA of existence and life. If we do not sing praise, the very stones will. But also, this God, in this story now moving boldly forward, will show a love such as never has been or will be seen. In the Book of Hebrews, we are told the humbling and touching truth that Jesus would later take even the Cross voluntarily, for joy: "For the . . . joy that was set before him endured the cross" (Heb 12:2). He would take the Cross for the Church, his bride, and all those he came to shine light on—we who sit in darkness and the shadow of death.

And so at this moment of all moments the narrative pauses for a song, a reflection to lend solemnity to the moment. This poem is canticle and more than canticle. As canticle it is the beginning of the "Gloria," and we sing it as we come before his holy presence each week for worship and the sacrament.

> Glory to God in the highest heaven
> and on earth peace among those whom he
> favors. (Lk 2:14)

But it is more than canticle; it is an affirmation. As such, it is also a subversive statement. When we sing or say it, we are agreeing with the angel who spoke that Jesus is the king and his kingdom is the true and everlasting one.

What we have come to call the angel choir more literally is "an army from heaven," or "soldiers from heaven." This canticle is not being sung by a group of chubby little fellows with wings who forgot to dress, or by a gaggle of ethereal women who have nothing solid or strong about them. I'm not sure our common representations of angels are on target. Actually, I'm pretty sure they are not; at least, it is hard to imagine angels that way in this moment.

No. Because here God is not only tweaking Caesar's nose, as it were, but in fact is giving notice that the empire's time is up. It is audacious, certainly, and yet that is the message. Yes, it will take a long time, and yes, its method will be surprising—a long and counterintuitive path that must go through Golgotha and the Cross and one single man's resurrection—but eventually Rome will be *both* converted and judged. In other words, though it will take a few hundred years, one might still say that eventually Jesus will defeat Rome both from within *and* from without; and though it takes the eyes of the Spirit to see it, still it is nothing short of amazing.

The Challenge of Christmas

If it seems an incredulous claim, consider what is perhaps the most surprising historical fact that ever has been. This baby was born of parents from a town so remote as to qualify as a place in the proverbial nowhere. The parents were poor, scurrying about because one of history's many tyrannical rulers said to. They were scurrying to a little town a handful of miles outside their home. Yet this baby born in the manger grew up to lead the most amazing movement that ever has existed, based upon love and forming out of diverse and differing people from all over the world one great family in faith. This baby grew up to give an equally audacious hope, and that hope has proven able to sustain itself through the generations, centuries, and indeed millennia. He began an ever-growing, ever-spreading family of God—today larger than ever, with one third of the world's population, over 2 billion—and it all began in one life that had such a humble and inconvenient beginning.[5] Let people make of it what they will; let cynics decry and skeptics harden their hearts.

And yet, of this much it would seem we can be sure: Jesus' birth night was not in historical reality any *more* glorious than Luke has told it. Say Luke made the angel part up, and his whole perspective of the Eternal Word being woven into time and history is all overdone or is the invention of an overromantic imagination. Say all of that, and then what you get would only make the surprising historical fact of Jesus' triumph and profound impact on history all the more *un*likely. Let that soak in for a moment, and then feel the burden of proof slowly beginning to shift to the other side, away from those who believe.

It is a curveball for the cynic: the obvious weaknesses, sicknesses, and failures in the Church through the ages only make the case of belief stronger. Because, yes, what a bunch of hypocrites we Christians are and have been throughout history. We follow One measured against whom we shall always fail—though that is no excuse and certainly not permission to give up trying. And yet that only goes to make it the more shocking and amazing that this thing of following Jesus has lasted so long, reached so far, and continues to grow.

There is a story that during the reign of Napoleon someone in great dismay rushed in to see the Vatican

Secretary of State, Cardinal Consalvi, and exclaimed, "Your Eminence, the situation is very serious. Napoleon wishes to destroy the Church." To which the wise old Cardinal is reputed to have wryly replied, "Not even we have succeeded in doing that!"[6]

The amazing reality is that from one perspective it can be argued that this little baby started a movement that defeated the empire—the greatest empire the world had seen by that time—from both inside and out, one might say. Defeat from the inside is a fact because by just after AD 300, Christianity—the religion of the "Christ ones," followers of the man this baby grew up to be—became the emperor's religion and a relatively short bit later was effectively named the empire's official religion. Whether the embattled would-be emperor, Constantine, was truly converted by a miracle sign in the skies, a sign from heaven, or whether he manipulated it all for political effect is beside the point. If the former, God did it in dramatic fashion. If the latter, it's all the more amazing that this movement of underlings and nobodies could shift the climate from their being unknown, to being mocked, to being persecuted, to eventually having enough grassroots support that an aspiring emperor would find claiming this religion to be politically expedient.

From the outside, the fall of Rome was foretold symbolically and figuratively in the Book of Revelation, chapters 17 and 18, as a pending judgment by God. And yes, of course, the fall did not happen because lightning bolts screamed from the heavens or an assertive angel army visited Rome and behaved in a manner a little more assertive than singing. The same prophets who foresaw God's visitation to earth in this baby also saw God's hand at work in and behind the political realities and changes of their day. Their understanding of God's interaction with and judgment upon empires was more nuanced and insightful than we might suppose. God, it seems, in some enigmatic way allows empires their day and will use their choices for his purposes while also reserving the right to bring his perfectly holy justice upon them later for those same acts. They, all the while unaware or in denial of the proverbial sword hanging over their souls, proceed on in their arrogance and understand it all as their own self-realization and glorification of their emperor, as a part of their great moment.[7]

At any rate, we have ranged a bit away from Luke's story, and whatever might be said of all of that, this much remains: inconspicuous though his birth was in the range of things that would count and be recorded in the telling of history to generations to come—this baby would become the man who affected history more than any other. Martin Luther King Jr. saw this and put it beautifully in one of his most famous sermons, "The Drum Major Instinct":

> He was born in an obscure village, the child of a poor peasant woman. And then he grew up in another obscure village, where he worked as a carpenter until he was thirty years old. Then for three years, he just got on his feet, and was an itinerant preacher. . . . He didn't have much. He never wrote a book. He never held an office. He never went to college. He

never visited a big city. He never went two
hundred miles from where he was born. . . .

Nineteen centuries have come and gone,
and today, he stands as the most influential
figure that ever entered human history. All of
the armies that ever marched, all the navies
that ever sailed, all the parliaments that ever
sat, and all the kings that ever reigned put
together have not affected the life of man on
this earth as much as that one solitary life.[8]

The subversive tenor of this passage parallels that of
the angels' militant words, but that aspect of the story has
largely been lost on us. It would not have been on Luke's
original audience. They would have grasped the audacious,
far-reaching, culture-shaping claim being made; even those
early Christians—without power, without pull, without yet
any visible evidence of any victory of their king beyond his
resurrection—would have grasped it.

Perhaps it is not surprising that there are no questions
in this scene, only praise. And that is what Christmas Day is
for—no matter how dark, or complex, or seemingly hope-
less the world may look or in fact be, this day stands as a
beacon on a rarefied high peak of history's long range of
valleys and ridges. I am reluctant to use the example, but let
us give credit where credit is due: Linus is right on spot in
the Peanuts "A Charlie Brown Christmas" when he (essentially) tells Charlie Brown to get his head up because the
events of this night are real and matter beyond whatever our

circumstances might be. Zechariah had already spoken of God's visitation and redemption even before this moment; in this moment they touch down. This much, and more, has been done and shall not be overthrown. The promised blessing in the angels' song gives peace and strength.

So the challenge that comes to us in this scene is to suspend our worries, fears, regrets, anxieties, and so on and join in the praise. That may be the biggest challenge we have yet faced: a conscious decision to put all that on hold, trust that good is coming to us, and lose ourselves in this moment. May we do as well with this day as did those humble shepherds. They turn out to make pretty decent disciples, at least at this point:

> And it came about as the angels went away from them into heaven, that the shepherds said to one another, "Let us go then up to Bethlehem and see this word which has come to be, which the Lord has made known to us." And they went hurrying and found Mary and Joseph and the newborn baby lying in the manger.
>
> Seeing this, they made known the things that had been spoken to them concerning this child. And all who heard were amazed concerning what was spoken to them by the shepherds. But Mary guarded all these words and pondered them in her heart. And the shepherds returned glorifying and praising God

about all they had heard and seen, [which
was] just as had been spoken to them. (Lk
2:15–20, AT)

The shepherds are so winsome! Once the angel choir is
done and the window to the heavens shuts, they act. They
go with haste and find Mary and Joseph and the baby, just
as they had heard. They are so excited that they cannot
hold it in! So they go and tell the news, and they return
to the same life for the meantime. Presumably nothing in
the fields has changed, and yet somehow they know that
everything is different. So they go glorifying and praising
God; they are lifted into places of joy and exhilaration.

Mary, for her part, continues as even more the ideal
disciple, a model of Christian faith. She has already made
the blanket offering of herself to God's purposes: "Let it be
done unto me according to your word," and when the angel
gave her news, she hurried to visit Elizabeth. Luke is telling
us that these are the things that people do when they want
to walk in step with the acts of God in the midst of life.

For Mary things are now moving ahead in her life at
a speed greater than she can sort out, yet she nonetheless
remains trusting. Traditionally her response to this surprising visit in the night is translated that she "treasured these
things and pondered them in her heart," and that lovely
language is on target. The first verb can mean "to preserve"
or "to protect," and the second literally means "to throw
together," or "to throw side by side." One commentator
argues—on the basis of occurrences of this (second) verb in
other nonbiblical Greek literature of the day—that this verb

is used to describe someone seeing the meaning in otherwise obscure events, often through divine help.[9] Maybe that is more than we can be confident was on Luke's mind here, but nonetheless the notion would seem to be consistent with the picture of Mary that Luke gives us. We translated this bit as "Mary guarded these things and pondered them in her heart." It is an endearing, heartfelt image, and along with the shepherds' return to their work, Luke thus begins to wind this scene down.

All that remains is for Luke to move someone off stage, which this time he does but with a half twist: "And when the eighth day was fulfilled he was circumcised and called the name Jesus, as named by the angel before he was conceived in the womb" (Lk 2:21, AT). This is closure, but only half so. The baby Jesus will stay on center stage for the next scene as well, since that scene follows closely in terms of the theme of introducing the Messiah, even as a baby, to the world and showing how heaven has long been weaving toward this One in this time.

The proximity of the next scene gives us a good excuse to remember that there are, joyfully, twelve days of Christmas including at least one Sunday of Christmas and often two. So we have one more chapter to walk this journey, one more scene Luke has for us, and one more canticle for us to ponder.

Keeping
the Story
Alive

If you are reading this chapter during the week following the first Sunday of Christmas, then likely what you are being wished by coworkers, neighbors, and friends is a "Happy New Year." I always reply "thank you and Merry Christmas!" It's a small thing but it does draw curious stares. And, of course, the wish of a "Happy New Year" is nice and well-intended, but I fight to keep it clear in my own mind and heart that that moment—a new year— came and passed five or so weeks ago, when we began this spiritual journey at the beginning of Advent. Advent is, of course, the beginning of the year in the Church's calendar, precisely because it is the time of preparation for remembering and celebrating God's visiting us in the incarnate form of a human being, which began when God arrived as an infant. And at this point, January 1 or not, we are still in Christmas, for there are, very happily, twelve days of Christmas, and well it deserves them!

Maybe it seems like splitting hairs, but I don't think so. My determination is not to let Black Friday and all it represents be the most important focus of my attention between Thanksgiving and Christmas, and not to let Christmas be swept away come December 26. This seems an important battlefront for my soul, for my identity. It is a battle concerning which story I understand myself to be a part of and holding on to that story even through the long passing of the years.

There is a poignant bit in the slightly dark humor of W. H. Auden's poem, "For the Time Being." In it he describes the effort often needed to pick up and carry on again after Christmas Day has passed because we are all exhausted from the hustle-bustle, overdoing the merriment, and because we have "attempted—quite unsuccessfully / To love all of our relatives, and in general / Grossly overestimated our powers." Auden continues to reflect more soberly that "to those who have seen / The Child, however dimly, however incredulously, / The Time Being is, in a sense, the most trying time of all."[1] So many trappings of joy and celebration are put away, and the rest of the culture carries on to the Next Big Distraction, which the marketing experts are careful to bring along promptly. There will be Super Bowl Sunday and shortly after that Valentine's Day: something for the manly man and something for the romantic woman.

But still we live and long for more—for a connection that is both deeper and wider than just whatever is happening this year. This is the great thing about the Church calendar: like New Year's Day or the Super Bowl or whatever else, the events of the Church calendar come around each year. Unlike all of those other events, the events in the Church calendar also mark and keep actual events that happened once in history, and have changed the course of, well, pretty much everything.

The Fulfillment of Time

So now let us circle back and recall that we began our spiritual journey in Advent. As we noted, Advent is not only about preparing to celebrate God's presence with us in the past, in the Incarnation of the Son of God; nor is it solely about God's presence with us through the Spirit in the present time—though wondrously it *is* about that presence, and indeed finding that presence anew has been the point of this spiritual journey. But Advent is also and perhaps best about looking forward to the time when God's presence will be with us—more properly, when we will be in *his* presence— unmitigated, unfiltered, with the knowledge of him and his glory covering all as the waters cover the seas; and God's glory will shine perfectly, pure, and clear.

This means that the time being is at some level always about waiting faithfully. Yes, it is also about acting with faith and courage and in keeping with God's calling to each one of us. God is kind to dignify us with a role to play; and our spiritual journey over these past weeks is meant to have shaped our understanding of that role for us, or given us greater courage or joy to put into doing our part.

But always in the midst of that there is also the reality that we are waiting the long wait for the return of Jesus to reign as king, and waiting is not something our culture has trained us to do. Quite the opposite: we have fast food, a commitment to convenience; smart phones and ever faster, ever more comprehensive access and "connectivity." Waiting is something we have implicitly learned to associate with hassle and indignation, as if we are being somehow disrespected.

But there is one more scene in the Christmas story in Luke that gives us two models to follow and two remarkable people who waited faithfully for a long time. They come on stage one after the other in the last scene before Jesus begins to grow up and to speak for himself, the last scene which involves the infant Jesus:

> When the time came for their purification according to the law of Moses, they [Mary and Joseph] brought him [the infant Jesus] up to Jerusalem to present him to the LORD (as it is written in the law of the LORD, "Every firstborn male shall be designated as holy to the LORD"), and they offered a sacrifice

> according to what is stated in the law of the
> LORD, "a pair of turtledoves or two young
> pigeons." (Lk 2:22–24)

Mary and Joseph brought Jesus to the Temple in Jerusalem to handle some Jewish rites that follow a birth, one regarding a firstborn son and the other the new mother. As Luke had already shown us, they are conscientious parents and have a living and real faith (for Mary we see this here, in Luke's gospel; for Joseph this shows more in Matthew's). The Law is more tender and forgiving than modern people typically assume: a mother was to offer a sheep as a sacrifice for purification, but "if she cannot afford a sheep, she shall take two turtle-doves or two pigeons" (Lv 12:8a). Apparently God did not choose to check himself into a luxury resort, so to speak, but to identify with the vast majority of the world population, as a poor person. So they go to take care of things, and the first of our models for faithful waiting comes to the stage:

> Now there was a man in Jerusalem whose
> name was Simeon; this man was righteous
> and devout, looking forward to the consola-
> tion of Israel, and the Holy Spirit rested on
> him. It had been revealed to him by the Holy
> Spirit that he would not see death before he
> had seen the LORD's Messiah. Guided by the
> Spirit, Simeon came into the temple; and
> when the parents brought in the child Jesus, to
> do for him what was customary under the law,
> Simeon took him in his arms. (Lk 2:25–28a)

"Righteous" is an adjective we've already met: Luke described Zechariah and Elizabeth as righteous, and that is good company for Simeon to keep. But as good as "righteous" is, "devout" would seem to be yet another step up; it is an adjective only Luke uses in all of the New Testament, and he uses it only four times. He uses it once here to describe Simeon and three times in the Book of Acts. The first is in Acts 2:5 to describe Jews gathered from all over the world for Pentecost—those to whom Peter will preach and many of whom will come to believe the good news about Jesus, about three thousand on that day. The next time the word is used is in chapter 8 when "devout men" buried the Church's first martyr, Stephen, who began a long (and still ongoing) company of martyrs. As they buried Stephen, they wept loudly over him: men of courage as well as devout in faith. And lastly, in chapter 22 this accolade describes Ananias, who had enough faith to follow the Spirit's instructions and go to Saul (when Saul was blind and still known as chief persecutor of the Church) and pray for him to be healed. In other words, to be "devout" was to be of good heart, ready to believe, and then to act openly and with courage.

And there is one more helpful bit on that word. The Old Testament prophecies of Micah alluded to the work of John the Baptist, and Luke has told a good bit of that story. There is one place in Micah where the prophet laments that "the faithful [devout] have disappeared from the land, and there is no one left who is upright" (Mi 7:2). Apparently that tide has turned in some sense as heaven has been working its weaving and bringing things to be, for now a devout one has come forward.

Simeon's righteous devotion is apparent in some sense by the fact that he has been "looking forward to the consolation of Israel." "Consolation" could be translated as "encouragement" or "comfort" and appears frequently in the Bible—but probably nowhere more well known than in its verbal form in the Old Testament in Isaiah 40, the passage that has been put into so many people's minds through the tenor recitative that begins the singing in Handel's *Messiah*:

> Comfort, O comfort my people,
>   says your God.
> Speak tenderly to Jerusalem,
>   and cry to her
> that she has served her term,
>   that her penalty is paid,
> that she has received from the LORD's hand
>   double for all her sins. (Is 40:1–2)

And presumably because of Simeon's piety and holy desires, "the Holy Spirit rested on him" and told him "that he would not see death before he had seen the LORD's Messiah." So "guided by the Spirit, Simeon came into the temple; and when the parents brought in the child Jesus, to do for him what was customary under the law, Simeon took him in his arms." Thus Luke draws up to the last canticle, but what is it this time that makes this moment so great that it needs pause for a song of reflection? The first of the canticles was the "Magnificat," and it had arguably the mildest moment leading to it of any of the three yet heard: it came in response to Elizabeth's exuberant exclamation and her relating to Mary that the child John had leapt in her womb at Mary's greeting. But is that really mild? Something powerful in the Spirit had happened, and there was a pause to reflect on what God was bringing together.

The second and third, the "Benedictus" and the "Gloria," had more obvious moments. The "Benedictus" was spoken when the miracle baby, John the Baptist, was born; Zechariah affirmed Gabriel's choice of name, and his tongue was set free to speak again—two miracles side by side, and on top of that the people's question that begged a response. The "Gloria" marks the most obvious of all; the angel-army choir sings at the moment when the weaving has become complete—the Incarnation had officially begun.

The Holy Spirit has urged Simeon to the Temple for this moment; verse 27 begins, "He came in the Spirit into the Temple." And this moment needs the depth of reflection in order to be sure that we, the readers, do not miss an important point: the child is a kind of hinge between the past from which he has come and the future that he will fulfill and bring. The past that Jesus will fulfill and bring to its completion is alluded to in the Law, mentioned three times in verses 22–24. This event takes place in the Temple, the place of God's presence, in order to fulfill requirements of that Law. This is a moment of God's creative work, and a renewed future is alluded to as the Spirit is mentioned three times in verses 25–27.[2]

The Canticle of Simeon

The three all come together in verse 27 as Luke sets up the canticle known as the "Nunc Dimittis": "Guided by the Spirit, Simeon came into the temple; and when the parents brought in the child Jesus, to do for him what was customary under the law, Simeon took him in his arms." The three come together in a wonderfully tender image, the old man taking the infant in his arms and speaking the canticle over him. He "praised God, saying,"

> Master, now you are dismissing your servant
> in peace,
>   according to your word;
> for my eyes have seen your salvation,
>   which you have prepared in the presence of
>   all peoples,
>   a light for revelation to the Gentiles
>   and for glory to your people Israel. (Lk 2:29–32)

In the West, the "Nunc Dimittis" has been sung in the night prayer service of Compline at least since the time of St. Benedict, in the early sixth century. Traditionally in the Catholic and Anglican traditions there is an accompanying antiphon that begins, "Into your hands, O LORD, I commend my spirit, for you have redeemed me, LORD God of truth." This antiphon leads into the "Nunc Dimittis," and then the canticle is followed with the collect: "Save us, O LORD, while waking, and guard us while sleeping, that awake we may watch with Christ and asleep may rest in peace." These are beautiful, evocative prayers that nicely resonate with the nuance of the early verses of the canticle and the sense of entrusting one's self fully into God's care and ultimate peace.

But also Simeon sees something of the new future the child will bring: the salvation that has been prepared in the sight of all peoples, light for revelation to the Gentiles, and glory for Israel. During his years of waiting, Simeon must have read the book of the prophet Isaiah. The book must have been one of his favorites for meditation, and apparently his open intimacy with God's Spirit had molded his heart and given him insight to see beyond the usual assumptions. Though Simeon is not quoting Isaiah directly, his vision has resonance with some of that great prophet's foretellings of the Messiah, especially the more stirring ones that come in the latter chapters of the book. For instance, Isaiah 42:6 and 49:6 speak of the Messiah as a light to the Gentiles, and like Simeon's vision, each passage is beautiful and breathtaking in scope.[3] Examine the specific verses that have the phrase about light to the nations:

> I am the LORD, I have called you in righteousness,
>> I have taken you by the hand and kept you;
> I have given you as a covenant to the people,
>> a light to the nations. (Is 42:6)

> It is too light a thing that you should be my servant
>> to raise up the tribes of Jacob
>> and to restore the survivors of Israel;

> I will give you as a light to the nations,
>> that my salvation may reach to the end of the
>> earth. (Is 49:6)

The concept of the nations, the Gentiles, being brought into God's salvation was therefore not new, but there is a difference between something existing in some distant and only imagined future and that same concept starting to become real. Sometimes when the reality comes to be, it is not quite the way people had imagined it. Perhaps the Gentiles would be saved, but only after their clear submission to the Law, and so on.

But here Simeon sees that this child is for all peoples, is a "light *for revelation* to the Gentiles" (same word as "nations")—which is a half measure more than "light to the nations."[4] In God incarnate those long-predicted but still abstracted realities would begin to take shape. Because this child was fulfilling the Law, was God's very presence, and would send the Spirit to spread the presence out wider than the Temple, that day when others begin to come into his presence would look different from what many had expected, and it would be more than many would be able to handle. The "Nunc Dimittis" may start off with a pastoral, genial image of ultimate peace, but it moves quickly to a disquieting image on a grandiose scale.

A Disturbing Prophecy

Apparently it was enough to unsettle Mary and Joseph. As Simeon turned his attention to them, he blessed them and gave them a second but not comforting word:

> And the child's father and mother were
> amazed at what was being said about him.
> Then Simeon blessed them and said to his
> mother Mary, "This child is destined for the
> falling and the rising of many in Israel, and
> to be a sign that will be opposed so that the
> inner thoughts of many will be revealed—
> and a sword will pierce your own soul too."
> (Lk 2:33–35)

The word translated as "destined" is more literally "laid down," with the sense of a foundation or something being put into place for a reason; heaven has woven this One into history at this time. But despite it being God's plan and presence, the path will not be easy. Yes, his presence will lead many in Israel to rise, but the harder flip side is stated first: he will be the reason many will fall. For the child will grow up to be a sign. This is another way of expressing a marker from beyond the veil, present in this world to point beyond this world; and this is another clue showing Simeon's having been shaped by the prophecies of Isaiah, for "sign" is a term that Isaiah uses considerably more than any other prophet.[5]

The presence of a sign from heaven can be either an occasion for joy or can be unsettling and provocative. Either way, it pushes past the veil and interrupts; it changes the agenda and puts things (otherwise pushed out into some abstracted future) on the table at the moment it is encountered. Does it indicate that what we have deep in our imaginations and attitudes is on board with heaven's point of view, or does it scandalize us to cry out, "How could God think *that*?" or, "What is God doing? Why would he do it *that* way?" Simeon sees that something about the child will scandalize, not only the people of Israel, but also the child's own mother.

As we see above, in English we tend to translate this word from Simeon such that the more general message about the child's effect on Israel and beyond is kept together, and then the particular word given to Mary is put at the end. It makes for easier reading, but it does not follow the order in which the original Greek text places these ideas. If we took the same translation just read but put the ideas in the same order as in the original text, the passage would go like this:

> This child is destined for the falling and the rising of many in Israel, and to be a sign that will be opposed—and a sword will pierce your own soul too—so that the inner thoughts of many will be revealed. (Lk 2:34b–35, author's arrangement)

It is a detail, but it matters. First, what is the sword that will pierce her heart? Traditionally it has been taken to mean the suffering Jesus will endure in the Passion, culminating in his very public and painful death on the Cross; and that would, of course, be a pain about as deep as any mother could endure, which seems to be the point here. The mysterious word of judgment spoken to the serpent all the way back in the Garden of Eden, considered to be the first hint of the Gospel or the good news of God finding a way to redeem his creation, will be fulfilled in the Passion:

> I will put enmity between you and the woman,
>   and between your offspring and hers;
> he will strike your head,
>   and you will strike his heel. (Gn 3:15)

Mystically minded and deep-seeing early Christians have taken Mary to be a kind of a second Eve, enabling the problems brought by the first Eve to be unwound through Mary's acceptance of the mission Gabriel gave to her. One of the most fervent and eloquent to express this idea was the fifth-century Syrian monk and priest, Jacob of Serug, who wrote many poems reflecting upon Mary's role in God's weaving of redemption into time and history. In one of these reflections on the annunciation, he mused:

> The evil time which had killed Adam was changed;
>   another good time came in which he would
>   be raised.
> Instead of a serpent, Gabriel rose to speak;
>   instead of Eve, Mary began to consent.[6]

But there would be lesser pains along the way to the Passion as well, including one found in Luke's next scene in which questions return to his gospel and on Mary's lips. When she confronts the young Jesus in the Temple after she and Joseph have been startled that he was not with them on their journey home from Jerusalem, Mary asks: "Child, why have you treated us like this? Look, your father and I have been searching for you in great anxiety." Jesus

answers her: "Why were you searching for me? Did you not
know that I must be in my Father's house?" (Lk 2:48–49).

Mary had been entrusted to steward the Word Made
Flesh, and her relationship to her son would be different
from what any normal mother might expect; indeed in the
visitation of the shepherds and the words of Simeon, that
difference has already begun. But in the next scene with
the exchange between mother and son, there is the beginning of a kind of a break: to whom does Jesus truly belong?
What is his mission and purpose in life, and how does he
see himself? Mary will have to let go in a sense far beyond
what every normal mother faces, difficult as the more normal route can be.[7]

But there is perhaps a stronger reason why the particular note to Mary comes when it does, rather than at the
end of Simeon's words. Simeon's last words are that "the
inner thoughts of many will be revealed." This is strong
language, almost a strong accusation against those with
"inner thoughts." "Inner thoughts" in the Bible does not
carry the positive sense for which we in our psychologiz-
ing era might use the term. It is not referring to some shy
person's secret affection for another or to creative ideas
lying deep inside us germinating until ready to take form.

No, the sense tends to be in another direction: the
idea is of people who perhaps appear fine, who know how
the social game is played, who consider themselves to be
upstanding, moral, and good citizens, but who actually at
some level are dissembling. Under the veneer is insecurity,
judgment, even hatred—all of which create resistance to

God's acts for redemption and a new community of love in his name. A quick look at the other places that the term (or the two words in close proximity and conceptual agreement) occurs in Luke will illustrate the sense. The first comes in Luke 5 when the four friends lower their paralyzed friend through the roof to get him to Jesus, and before healing him, Jesus tells the man his sins are forgiven (which throws the scribes and Pharisees into a tizzy). "When Jesus perceived their questionings, he answered them, 'Why do you raise such questions in your hearts?'" (Lk 5:22). The next use of the term happens on a Sabbath. The scribes and Pharisees are already watching to see if they can catch Jesus doing anything untoward, which seems only to have sharpened Jesus' resolve, for "even though he knew what they were thinking, he said to the man who had the withered hand, 'Come and stand here.' He got up and stood there" (Lk 6:8). Jesus, of course, then healed him.

Even among his own disciples, "inner thoughts" were a seedbed of envy: "An argument arose among them as to which one of them was the greatest. But Jesus, aware of their inner thoughts, took a little child and put it by his side" (Lk 9:46–47) and taught them a simpler, purer way. And among his own followers, after his resurrection, "inner thoughts" represent doubts. When he appeared to his followers, before showing them his hands and his feet, he said to them, "Why are you frightened, and why do doubts arise in your hearts?" (Lk 24:38).

The weaving that has begun and will continue in ever-greater texture and color as Jesus grows and begins his work will put people at a crossroad, force them to show their hand, and let their true selves come out. But these sorts of faithless and unloving "inner thoughts" are not in keeping with who we have seen Mary to be. Luke has shown her to us as an early model of a faithful person, so it seems right that the word to her is separated from this stronger, darker bit.

If Mary is a young woman whom Luke presents as a model of faithful discipleship, he has one other woman in a different life stage that serves as a model disciple as well. The prophet Anna together with Simeon form a pair of the "lowly" whom Mary reflected on in the "Magnificat." They have been lifted up, in a manner of speaking, as they are put before us as models of faithful waiting over the long years of life.

> There was also a prophet, Anna the daughter of Phanuel, of the tribe of Asher. She was of a great age, having lived with her husband seven years after her marriage, then as a widow to the age of eighty-four. She never left the temple but worshiped there with fasting and prayer night and day. At that moment she came, and began to praise God and to speak about the child to all who were looking for the redemption of Jerusalem. (Lk 2:36–38)

It is possible to translate the phrase describing her age in another way, to read "as a widow for eighty-four years." If that were the case, then she would have been married for seven years, widowed for eighty-four years. Add to that however old she was upon marriage (most likely young by modern standards), and she would have been over one hundred years old when she found the Holy Family there in the Temple! Either way, she has lived long and the great majority of her years as a widow, which may give some hint as to why Luke was keen to include her in his careful telling of the Gospel story.

To be a widow has never been easy, and especially in the ancient world it could be precarious. Luke, with his special concern for vulnerable peoples, mentions widows in his gospel ten times (compare to only six references in the other three gospels combined). The early Church would privilege widows as a class of people deserving care, as Luke would tell in Acts 6, and the Church would have to wrestle with how to care for them well and appropriately.[8] Anna is the ideal widow, representing someone who has passed the years in pursuit of God with her body, mind, and soul, and who has love to share with others. So when she happened upon Simeon and the family, she began to praise God and—another disciple similar to the shepherds—to share the news with anyone who would hear it.

After Simeon's stronger and more foreboding words, Anna's are a bright ending to the scene in the Temple. Then it is time for Luke to wrap up the scene, having made the points about the hinge of history that this child is. So Luke sends the Holy Family off stage, as it were, while Jesus continues to live into the weaving.

> When they had finished everything required
> by the law of the LORD, they returned to

> Galilee, to their own town of Nazareth. The
> child grew and became strong, filled with
> wisdom; and the favor of God was upon him.
> (Lk 2:39–40)

Keeping the Story Alive in Us

What does this scene mean for us as we near the closure of the spiritual journey we have undertaken these past weeks? How do Simeon and Anna teach us to wait faithfully and actively for the glorious fulfillment of all the things begun in God's weaving in the Incarnation and continued through the lives and work of his people through the years since? Or, put another way, what do they show us about having our lives come along into the warp and woof of what God is and has been doing, that we might be a strand working with the pattern?

Not to overdo it, but it does seem we can pull three threads from their example. The first would be to be people who keep the story we are living by being faithful in prayer, in fasting, and in worship. In other words, be like Anna. Be faithful in personal spiritual disciplines and in worship together with the Church, with the goal of growing intimate with the Spirit (as was Simeon), that we might know God deeply and vibrantly in the here and now. The next thread, to generalize a little on an example from Simeon, would be to have the perception and pastoral sensitivity that he had when he blessed Mary, Joseph, and the baby—in other words, simply to notice, love, and care for others. And the last borrows from Anna's example again: to overflow with joy and anticipation and spread the news around.

This last thread is another of Luke's great passions. Luke wrote his gospel and the Acts—writing more of the New Testament than any other writer—and their length suggests he wrote them as a transportable pair of scrolls, a summary kit including everything one would need in order to take the Gospel around the world. It is more than we can go into here, but the books of Luke and of Acts basically have the same overall literary form in terms of how the story builds and is resolved, and are the same length (one standard scroll in their day).[9] He wrote a paired kit ready-made for traveling merchants to take along that they might share the news.

To write these books must have been one of Luke's great passions, because he saw it as it is—as a weaving that had its beginning in heaven. Theologians came to call this the "*missio Dei*"—the "mission of God"—and to point out that the first move was God's, weaving himself into time and history in the Incarnation. Simeon talks it up as "a light for revelation to the Gentiles"; and Anna, in her own way and in her own circle of influence, begins to carry it forward, spontaneously, and in joy. To be offered the opportunity to take God's mission forward is a privilege, but as Simeon saw, it was not easy. But it is beautiful and worthwhile.

Going Ahead with Courage and in Joy

O ur spiritual journey began roughly six weeks ago, if you are reading this near the feast of the Epiphany, the official end of the Christmas season. Six weeks is not, in the grand scheme of reckoning, a long time. But on the other hand, it is longer than a month, more than a tenth of a year, and long enough to see new things or to see things anew.

If you have been journaling through this journey, it may be a good time now to go back and look through what you've written. What has God brought to mind in these weeks? Where has he been focused to work in and on and with you? In what ways do you want to live differently? Into what new paths and patterns do you want to move? What things to you want to thank God for showing you or teaching you over the course of this journey? Or for what things do you want to thank him for giving you comfort or a new lens for seeing them?

Maybe this "holiday season" that has just passed has been an easy and fun one; here's hoping it has. But maybe it has been challenging or saddening; if that is the case, here's hoping this journey has given you a measure of consolation for today and a bright hope for the days and years to come.

Or maybe this is the first time you have ever taken the Bible seriously, or have ever read it this way—more slowly, with attention to what is going on with the characters, how the story relates to the rest of the scriptures and to God's overall purpose, or how it may keep its own integrity and at the same time come across the cultures and centuries to speak to your own life circumstances. If so, praise God! And isn't it amazing? Maybe you will have a hunger for more of the scriptures, which are food for our souls.

Strictly speaking we ought to have gone on and finished Luke chapter 2 by looking at verses 41–52, the story about Jesus as a boy when he stays back at the Temple in Jerusalem after Mary and Joseph have already started for home. We alluded to it—only just—in the last chapter, but that is all. But also it is the seventh scene in Luke's gospel that comes before Jesus is an adult, going public with his work. Therefore in terms of the literary structure of Luke's gospel, it really should be in with the six scenes through which we have walked. Besides that, seven, of course, is the biblical number of wholeness, and ancient authors tended to pay attention to things like that, as, presumably, did their audiences.

And, alas, the four questions in Luke's gospel before the birth match nicely with the four weeks (or partial fourth week) of Advent. The two scenes of the infant Jesus (the birth and the presentation) match nicely with the (basically) two weeks of Christmas. This scene has something of the feel of Epiphany about it conceptually (though, of course, properly in the Church calendar Epiphany is the province of the Magi, of Jesus' baptism, or of Jesus turning the water into wine). Epiphany is about the revealing of Jesus' glory, and arguably this moment in the Temple is the first moment that his glory began to leak through, as it were.

It happens as the questions return here in Luke's gospel. Mary asks the next one: "Child, why have you treated us like this? Look, your father and I have been searching for you in great anxiety" (Lk 2:48).

And then Jesus answers her with a question of his own: "Why were you searching for me? Did you not know that I must be in my Father's house?" (Lk 2:49).

John Donne caught a glimpse of the glory shining through in this scene, and expressed it poignantly:

Temple

> With His kind mother, who partakes thy woe,
> Joseph turn back; see where your child doth sit,

> Blowing, yea blowing out those sparks of wit,
> Which Himself on the doctors did bestow.[1]

But for all that, we have not given this scene full treatment. The scene is transitional—it opens up as much of a new horizon as it closes the section through which we have been walking—and in that sense it is not a great one for ending a journey but is a great one for picking up from here and starting another journey. By the time one gives it the treatment it deserves, one's mind has begun to venture off to the new horizon to which it points.

But be that as it may, its two questions can be felt to resonate deeply with the angst of people in the world today who long to sort out whither or whether God is; in exasperation we say to God, "We have been searching for you in great anxiety!" In one very real sense God replies, "I have given you a long story that I have been working out for generations, centuries, indeed millennia, and you will find me walking there." And if we dig in and hear the voice of Jesus and the Spirit he sends to us illuminating the path, then his glory shines out, we are amazed, and we find rest for our souls.

It does not do that scene justice to say so little, but Luke's brilliance as an author and his narrative structure seem to deserve at least that little touch of nominal closure. And it lets us see that questions have returned to Luke's gospel. Questions will be scattered throughout the rest of the path, for one of Jesus' primary ways of responding to people who approached him was to ask them questions. I think it had something to do with the manner in which he functioned as a sign to reveal the inner thoughts of people; at least that is what tended to happen in those moments.

But for now it only remains to recall that in the first scene of Luke's gospel Zechariah the priest was having the greatest day of his career, and also was getting overwhelmed and surprised beyond what he could handle. He was struck dumb by the angel Gabriel, and that meant that when he went out to face the people who were waiting outside, he was unable to offer them the traditional Levitical blessing that a priest was expected to give upon completion of the sacrifice. That was a loose end that has stayed open and frayed since, in a way. Would the blessing ever be given, and to whom?

Luke picked this loose end up at the end, in the closure of the last scene of his gospel, and the blessing was given[2]:

> Then he [Jesus] led them out as far as Bethany, and, lifting up his hands, he blessed them. While he was blessing them, he withdrew from them and was carried up into heaven. And they worshiped him, and returned to Jerusalem with great joy; and they were continually in the temple blessing God. (Lk 24:50–53)

I hope his blessing has come to you during this journey. May it remain with you always.

Notes

Introduction

1. In terms of length. The Gospel of Luke and the Book of Acts are attributed to him and together amount to the longest contribution of any author to the New Testament.

The First Week of Advent

1. Raymond Brown, *The Birth of the Messiah* (New York: Doubleday & Co., 1977), 259–60.

2. Ibid.

3. Origen, "Commentary on John," in *The Ante-Nicene Fathers, Translations of the Writings of the Fathers down to A.D. 325*, 5th ed., vol. 10, ed. Allan Menzies (Grand Rapids, MI: Wm. B. Eerdmans, 1951), 359.

4. Clement of Alexandria, *Exhortation to the Greeks*, trans. G. W. Butterworth (New York: G. P. Putnam's Sons, 1919), 25.

The Second Week of Advent

1. NRSV except my italics and insertion of literal translation for the word at issue: *episkiazw*.

2. Donne, of course, understood that Mary did not literally make Jesus, who was rather "begotten, not made" as the

145

Creed affirms, but he could not resist the paradox of God's embodied presence in such small and, as it were, primal space, and delighted to bring that paradox to light through what was the fashion of his day, a poetic fashion called "wit." I included verses 1–2, 5–6a, 12–14 of "Annunciation," the second of the seven interlinked, holy sonnets of which the overall work is titled "La Corona."

John Donne, *John Donne: The Complete English Poems*, ed. C. A. Patrides (London: J. M. Dent, 1985), 336–37.

The Third Week of Advent

1. In the singular.

2. Hugh Henry, "Magnificat," in *The Catholic Encyclopedia*, vol. 9 (New York: Robert Appleton, 1910), accessed September 24, 2011, from *New Advent*, www.newadvent.org/cathen/09534a.htm.

3. Dietrich Bonhoeffer, *Prisoner for God: Letters and Papers from Prison* (New York: Macmillan, 1959), 165.

The Fouth Week of Advent

1. Brown, *Birth of the Messiah*, 384.

2. Ibid., 386.

3. Even to suggest it here sounds audacious, but we will pick this up in more detail later. See also Brendan Byrne, *The Hospitality of God: A Reading of Luke's Gospel* (Collegeville, MN: The Liturgical Press, 2000), 28–29. Byrne suggests a way to understand how the salvation spoken of here would eventually lead to political change.

4. The NRSV translation is the same except for the "yet even" in the first line, but the "even" matters because of there

being both "*kai*" and "*de*" around the emphatic personal pronoun—i.e., three words where technically just one ("*kai*") would do to produce "and."

5. Brown, *Birth of the Messiah*, 373.

6. This one gets a little complicated so it has been relegated to the notes. Basically there are Old Testament predictions of the "branch of the house of David" in which "branch" got translated in the ancient Greek version of those scriptures with the Greek word used here (Zechariah 3:8 and 6:12), which can reflect a branch shooting out and up, but more commonly it means a dawn or sunrise. There are pointed references to the Messiah as a star rising (Numbers 24:17 is a great one), which are conceptually similar and which are forerunners, of course, of the star in Matthew's gospel that will attract the Wise Men, but those have a different Greek word. Also there is a reference in an extrabiblical Jewish sacred writing that is conceptually similar on the "branch" side, looking to "the sprout of the God Most High," from "Testament of Judah" (24:4).

Brown, *Birth of the Messiah*, 373–74, 390.

Christmas Day

1. Joel B. Green, *The Gospel of Luke* (Grand Rapids, MI: Wm. B. Eerdmans, 1997), 125.

2. Howard Foster Lowry and Willard Thorp, eds., *An Oxford Anthology of English Poetry* (New York: Oxford, 1956), 247.

3. Brown, *Birth of the Messiah*, 415–16.

4. Ibid, 424.

5. The Pew Forum on Religion and Public Life, *Global Christianity: A Report on the Size and Distribution of the World's Christian Population* (December, 2011), accessed January 12, 2012, www.pewforum.org/Christian/Global -Christianity-exec.aspx.

6. Timothy Radcliffe tells this story at the end of his book, *What is the Point of Being a Christian* (New York: Burns and Oates, 2005), 212.

7. Yes, it is a complex reality and a big claim to make. See for instance Isaiah 5:26–30 and 7:18–20 for God "whistling" for a foreign empire to do his work of judgment. Then examine Isaiah 14:25, 30:31, 52:4 for God bringing judgment upon that empire, and then Isaiah 19:23 for a vision of a day when members of even that empire (and those empires) will come together in peace to worship the living God together.

8. Martin Luther King Jr., "The Drum Major Instinct," in *A Testament of Hope: The Essential Writings and Speeches of Martin Luther King, Jr.*, ed. James M. Washington (San Francisco: Harper Collins, 1986), 266.

9. Brown, *Birth of the Messiah*, 406–7, citing the work of W. C. van Unnik.

The Twelve Days of Christmas

1. John Hollander and J. D. McClatchy, eds., *Christmas Poems (Everyman's Library Pocket Poets)* (New York: Alfred A. Knopf, 1999), 221–22.

2. Brown, *Birth of the Messiah*, 452–53. Brown points out the confluence here of the three streams: Law, Temple, and Spirit.

3. Ibid., 458.

4. Byrne, *Hospitality of God*, 35 (italics added).

5. Isaiah uses the word/image fifteen times, nearly once in every 2000 words. Jeremiah is a distant second, at eight occurrences spread out in every 4000 words. Ezekiel is next, at six occurrences only once every 5000+ words. See, for instance, Isaiah's first two uses, in 7:11 and 7:14, and his last use, in 66:19.

6. Jacob of Serug, *On the Mother of God*, trans. Mary Hansbury (Crestwood, NY: St. Vladimir's Seminary Press, 1998), 29.

7. Byrne, *Hospitality of God*, 36.

8. See Acts 6 and 1 Timothy 5:1–15.

9. The first points here are easy enough to sort out. The last one, about each book being the length of a scroll of that time, I picked up in seminary, but I cannot remember from whence or whom.

Conclusion

1. The first four verses of "Temple," the fourth of the seven interlinked sonnets of "La Corona." John Donne, *John Donne, The Complete English Poems*, ed. C.A. Patrides (London: J.M. Dent, 1985), 337.

2. Brown, *Birth of the Messiah*, 280.

Timothy Clayton is the rector of Christ the Redeemer Anglican Church on the Boston North Shore. He grew up in the Charlotte area and earned his bachelor's degree from the University of North Carolina at Chapel Hill. He spent time teaching English in Budapest, Hungary, and later graduated with high honors from Gordon-Conwell Theological Seminary.

Clayton founded a Christian community in Portland, Maine, and a church in Charlotte, North Carolina, and has led missions and spiritual pilgrimages to more than a dozen countries on five continents. So far his favorite places on earth are Lindisfarne, Durham Cathedral in England, and the Masai Mara in Kenya. Clayton resides near his church with his wife and three children.

Founded in 1865, Ave Maria Press,
a ministry of the Congregation of
Holy Cross, is a Catholic publishing
company that serves the spiritual and
formative needs of the Church and its
schools, institutions, and ministers;
Christian individuals and families; and
others seeking spiritual nourishment.

For a complete listing of titles from

Ave Maria Press

Sorin Books

Forest of Peace

Christian Classics

visit www.avemariapress.com

ave maria press® / Notre Dame, IN 46556
A Ministry of the United States Province of Holy Cross